"Jack Zenger's new book is chock-full of practical how-tos and watch-outs. He does an outstanding job of introducing the basic concepts involved in performance enhancement and also provides a clear, well-organized framework for anyone interested in achieving substantial improvements in their performance. With this book, Zenger performs an important service to the business community. I recommend it wholeheartedly to executives, managers, salespeople, and others interested in achieving peak performance."

Charles Garfield, Ph.D.
Author of *Second to None* and *Peak Performance*

"This is a fun, easy-to-read, and very practical book. It combines the best of Zenger Miller's strength in condensing extensive research into "how to" steps with Jack's warmth, wisdom, and experience."

Jim Clemmer
Author of *Firing on All Cylinders* and *Pathways to Performance*

"Jack Zenger has crafted what every senior officer longs for—a practical, easy-to-understand guide for frontline employees wanting to improve their personal productivity."

Daryl R. Conner
Author of *Managing at the Speed of Change*

Not Just for CEOs

SURE-FIRE SUCCESS SECRETS
FOR THE LEADER
IN EACH OF US

Jack Zenger

IRWIN
Professional Publishing®
Chicago • London • Singapore

Times Mirror
Higher Education Group

Library of Congress Cataloging-in-Publication Data
Zenger, John H.
    Not just for CEOs : sure-fire success secrets for the leader in each of us / Jack Zenger.
       p.   cm.
    Includes index.
    ISBN 0-7863-0528-2
    1. Labor productivity. 2. Strategic planning. 3. Performance standards. 4. Career development. I. Title.
HD57.Z43   1996
650.1—dc20   95–25890

Printed in the United States of America
1 2 3 4 5 6 7 8 9 0 BP 2 1 0 9 8 7 6 5

The person who grabs a cat by the tail learns 44% more about cats than the person who reads about, or merely observes them.

—Robert Beggs

Introduction

Who's This Book For?

Everyone who works inside an organization. It's not just for
CEOs or managers. It's especially written for the frontline—the
salespeople, customer service reps, accountants, factory workers,
administrative assistants, engineers, receptionists, and machine
operators—in any company or government agency. And not
because they are the cause of most organization's problems. It's
because frontline employees offer the most potent solution.

In the past, the higher up you went, the more responsible you'd
feel. Now, people at all levels have learned they've got to care.
Their jobs are at stake. They can't leave the success and survival
of the organization solely up to the executives.

This book tells you how *you* can make a difference inside your
organization. It is a message that every CEO wishes were understood and practiced by every frontline person in the organization.

Why Should I Read It?

Organizations are going through dizzying changes. Problems
stemming largely from inefficient systems and bad management
practices in the past are so complex that everyone must help find
solutions to them.

The problems can only be fixed when everyone accepts account-
ability to be part of that solution.

If you read this book and apply it, you will unleash your
abilities, you'll smile more at work, others will view you as

"indispensable," and you will be one of those people who honestly can say, "I made a difference." Whether or not the organization has designated you as a leader, this book shows you how you can be a big part of making your organization soar.

What Will I Get Out of It?

This book offers specific ideas about improving your personal productivity. Lots of them will seem like common sense, but unfortunately most of us get our full load of common sense late in life. You'll get no ivory tower theory. There are no fancy diagrams or models. No academic jargon. Just distilled wisdom.

The book uncovers the specific behaviors of top performers at all levels inside an organization. It describes what makes them so effective and details the specific steps you can take to follow their path, and adds some tips on how to do it.

Why Is Productivity Emphasized?

Productivity is the most important issue facing us today.

• For the individual, it determines job security, because organizations can afford to keep only highly productive people.

• For the company, it dictates whether the company stays in business, grows, and competes with other firms. Plug in the annual productivity increase and economists can tell you what salary increases companies can afford. That in turn tells you the house or apartment you'll live in, the car you drive, the vacation you can take, and how often you eat out. There's just no way a company can continually pay higher salaries and provide better benefits unless people inside produce more. It's that simple.

- For our nation, productivity gains determine our standard of living. If our productivity gains since 1970 had been as high as the decades before that, we would all have a 25 percent better standard of living.

Studies have shown that most of us want to be productive. The frontline people complain that management won't give them the resources and the freedom to be more productive. That's true, and increasingly management is learning to get out of the way of well-motivated frontline staff.

Where Did These Ideas Come From?

First, these ideas came from combing through the published research on productivity, then from talking with leading experts. Add to that decades of experience in working with organizations in training frontline associates. Finally, I've added my experience as an executive, as a college professor, and as a consultant.

The book also contains ideas and examples from many Zenger Miller associates, people whose work demonstrates unusual personal productivity.

How Should I Read This Book?

Don't just speed-read this book. If you race through, and then shelve it, little or nothing will happen. Take one chapter at a time. Devour the content. Put it into practice. Don't go on to the next chapter until you've done something about the one you just finished. Treat the book like a manual telling you how to build something. There's no need to go on to the end if the steps in the middle haven't been done. Put emphasis on those sections where you have the most to gain.

Becoming a more productive person means putting these principles into practice. If you don't have these skills now, you'll get them the same way an athlete or musician gets their skill—practice, practice, and more practice.

Can Some Groups Benefit More Than Others?

Some facts are useful in answering this question:

Changes in productivity.

In the past 30 years, manufacturing has increased its productivity by 18 percent, while office productivity during that same time has gone down 2 percent.

Absolute levels of productivity.

Most experts believe that office productivity tends to be the lowest of all groups inside organizations, while factory workers are the highest, and the "knowledge workers" (accountants, engineers, chemists, designers) are in between.

Industry differences

Some industries have had low or no productivity growth over the past decade. These include software, retailing, healthcare, food products, transportation, restaurants, entertainment, insurance, real estate, and construction.

Service sector versus manufacturing

Service oriented work doesn't use technology and machinery to drive their processes, so it has a higher labor component. Service-sector jobs are now 79 percent of the employment in North America. Productivity gains in the service sector have been roughly half that of the increases in manufacturing productivity.

So, who can benefit the most?

At first it would seem that those whose productivity is low or not increasing would be the groups to target. But the best get better, and all groups can benefit. In theory, those who start from the lowest base should show the greatest growth in productivity. Historically, however, it has been just the opposite.

We conclude that the opportunities for improvement are endless and they are available to everyone.

Acknowledgments

Special thanks go to Barry Schwenkmeyer, who gave extra-ordinary assistance in the writing of early drafts. Thanks also to a number of colleagues at Zenger Miller who graciously contributed examples and ideas to this book: Jennifer Berkley, Christine Crawford, Randie Guest, Melinda Hunt, Cindy Johansson, Maureen Kelly, Marilynn Milligan, and Judy Stipancic. Robin Zenger Baker also made valuable suggestions for the final manuscript.

Dedication

This book is dedicated to my father, John Henry Zenger (1900–1994), who constantly strove to improve himself and the world about him, and to Holly, my wife, who has perfected the ability to be productive and blend it with having fun.

CONTENTS

PART ONE
HOW TO STREAMLINE YOUR JOB

Here's a news flash: You were not hired because your organization wanted another person on the payroll. You were hired because of some important work it wants you to do.

But *what* work? If you are like most people, your job is becoming more complex. You may be finding it harder and harder to figure out what you do—or what you *should* do. There are probably days when it feels as if you're expected to do everything.

Successful people have learned how to stay on top of their jobs. That's because they thoroughly analyze their jobs and organize them to eliminate unnecessary steps or wasted effort. They look around for others who have developed clever ways of doing things. They construct job aids to help them do their jobs more effectively. They realize time is their most precious resource and seek ways to speed everything they handle. They also realize that they were hired not just to do their jobs, but to constantly figure out ways to do them better. Finally, the highly productive people wage war on waste, knowing that it is an arch-enemy of every organization.

Chapter 1

Be a Calculating Person

The popular press recently reported that a large hotel chain had been wrestling with delays in getting rooms ready for new guests. A key executive finally tackled the issue. After collecting information about the problem, he discovered that the problem wasn't a lack of well-trained service personnel, nor was it their reluctance to work hard. It all boiled down to a lack of towels. Chambermaids were waiting for the towels to be taken to the laundry, washed and dried, and then brought back to the floors. But until someone measured the time delays and collected information on the causes, the problem wouldn't go away.

I have been struck by the incredible variety of activities that can be measured and consequently streamlined.

For example, here are a few work processes our clients have made more efficient by measuring them and cutting away unnecessary steps:

• **Time to repair circuit boards.** The company reduced it from 11 to 5 days.

• **Time to bill hospital patients for in-patient services.** The hospital reduced it by one day simply by improving the coding process in medical records.

• **Golf course utilization.** Golfers complained about the time it was taking to play one round. By collecting specific information to find the causes for delays, the company improved directions given to golfers, streamlined scheduling, and fixed some of the fairways. This reduced complaints to zero, while significantly increasing the number of golfers on the course.

• **Time to respond to inquiries about orders.** The company reduced the time from three days to one hour.

• **Snowmobile utilization.** Customers were concerned about the speed and safety of snowmobiles. The company was faced with needing to buy more snowmobiles because of their down time in maintenance. Collecting data led to better education of the customers on how to use them and improved maintenance (including preventive maintenance). This reduced complaints to virtually none and eliminated the need to buy more snowmobiles.

• **Time to process orders in a school district.** Delivery of orders went from 4 days to 3.5 hours.

• **Cost of tests on newly admitted patients in a hospital.** By collecting information on the tests each physician was ordering and making that information available to the medical director, the hospital was able to reduce unnecessary tests and not exceed the costs for which it would be reimbursed.

What a wonderful variety of issues! And what success in making things better. Measurement is like a searchlight that you turn on a problem. Not only do you see it more clearly, but the very act of measurement unleashes forces that help solve the problem.

"All facts are friendly."
—Robert H. Waterman, Jr.

Here's a snap quiz. Circle Y for Yes, N for No, or DK for Don't Know.

1. I am spending my time on the job well. (Y / N / DK)

2. I am getting good results. (Y / N / DK)

3. My performance has improved over this time last year. (Y / N / DK)

You may have a general sense of how well you're doing (although these days you may not). But you'll never really know and you'll never be able to prove it to anybody else unless you measure the work you do.

One reason we periodically measure children's height on the same wall is to help them get a sense of how much—and how fast—they're growing.

Establishing objective measures of your work tips you off to changes much earlier than casual observation.

Highly successful people always know how they're doing, because they measure their work. When you measure your work, you get hard facts. These facts tell you things like:

• How long it takes to complete a certain task (you may be surprised).

• Which tasks give you the biggest headaches—for example, having to wait around, do things twice, correct other people's errors, or work with bad materials or information.

• Whether you're spending your time on the right tasks—the tasks that create successes for you and your company.

Quantifying what you do and how you spend your time increases your understanding of your job. With that greater understanding come greater self-confidence and a sense of mastery.

Some people think it's a waste of time to measure their work, because it's "too unstructured." Or because they don't think they have much control over what they do.

But you may find when you measure your work that it's more structured than you think. You'll see patterns you'd like to strengthen—or change.

Also, facts are powerful. Even if you're the CEO, they're more powerful than your opinions. When you've got the facts, you can go to your boss and say, "Did you know I spend 42 percent of my time preparing reports and checking other people's

work, and only 15 percent of my time dealing with customers?"
Or, "I find the cost of the errors is far less than the cost of my
time in finding them."

Without the facts, you can still ask your boss to change
your duties. But it may sound a lot like whining.

**If you personally owned your company, would you
eliminate any of the things you do? Any reports?
Approvals? Paperwork? Tasks? If so, act like an owner
and do your best to get them removed now.**

What You Can Do

What you measure will depend on your job. Don't measure
something just because it's easy to measure. That's like looking
for your watch where the light is good instead of where you lost
it. The most important things may be harder to measure. But
nearly everything can be measured if you use some ingenuity.
Aim for those measures that will help you make improvements
and predict your future success. Tracking what's happened in the
past can be revealing, but the most valuable measures are those
that anticipate what will happen days or weeks ahead.

1. List the most important outputs you produce. How
   do you measure them? If you don't, how could
   you? Make a chart or other visual device to display the results.

2. For two or three days, keep a log of everything you
   do and how long each activity takes. What patterns
   do you observe? What distractions could you get
   rid of? How much time does it take you to get the
   information you need?

3. Keep a record of your phone calls. Who do you talk to? For how long?

4. Measure your work in terms of the results that are important to your organization. For example, if you're in sales, how many telephone calls does it take you to get an appointment with a customer? How many appointments for a written proposal? How many written proposals for a sale?

5. Make a list of the work steps you have to repeat unnecessarily. Note any patterns or reasons.

6. Keep track of how long it takes you to give people the information they ask you for. How often do you need to get back to them later? How much later? (This is especially critical if you're dealing with customers.)

7. Find out the things you do that are most important to your customers. Measure them in terms your customers would use: number of errors or time to completion.

8. Keep track of your own batting average in keeping the commitments you've made.

 Tips from the Highly Successful

• **Use a checksheet.** A checksheet is simply a form that lets you record information in whatever way you want to—as check-marks, numerical measures, or brief comments. Make one that's easy to use, and keep it close at hand so you'll have it when you need it.

• **Put your data to work.** Take a good look at the information you've collected about your work. What does it mean? What should happen next? Who needs to be involved? What can *you* do right now?

- **Make your data stand out.** These days most of us live with information overload. If you want people to pay attention to your data, put it in graphic form. There are many kinds of graphs. Choose the one that makes your point. The fact that you take the time to measure your own work sends a clear message to your boss and others that you care. You want to make a difference in your organization.

Chapter 2

Look at Your Job Sideways

A s part of a home remodeling project, it became clear that we needed more electric power. (When the freezer went on, the lights in my office would dim.) I took the construction plans to the electric power company, which promptly lost them. After six weeks of delay I was told that it would be a month before they could bring in the new wiring. I finally threatened to contact the Public Utilities Commission. Within hours a crew was scheduled to come out to dig the trench, lay the new pipe, and pull the necessary wires from the power pole. The work was to take place the next day, but this had already caused a costly delay in the overall project.

The charming young woman who called to tell me that the crew would be there the next day said, just as our conversation was ending, "Oh, by the way, did you by any chance want to have this power *connected?*"

A few moments went by, and I confess to having some flippant, some sarcastic, and some irate thoughts. Then it dawned on me that she was really trying to help me.

"Of course I'd like it connected," I said in my calmest voice.

"Well, we're the construction department, and the connection is done by our operations group. I'm not supposed to do this, but if you'd like, I'll call them for you and make arrangements to have it connected."

"Thank you, thank you," I said.

This electric utility was organized for its own convenience, with departments that each had responsibility for doing one thing. The woman who called me realized that the "real work" occurred between departments, and so she took it upon herself to look at her job horizontally. That's how customers can best be served.

Highly successful people focus on what's good for the total organization and its customers, not just their department. To do this, they have learned how to look at their jobs sideways.

Organizations still maintain departments—sales, marketing, accounting, engineering, manufacturing, and so forth—and they still set performance goals for them. But the fact is, most work takes place horizontally across traditional departmental boundaries. Think about it. Someone in manufacturing, for example, works with someone in purchasing, who works with someone in finance, who works with someone in shipping and receiving, and so on.

When problems occur, they usually happen at the hand-off points between departments. These are sometimes called "white spaces" because they fall outside the boxes on an organization chart. White spaces are no-man's lands where nobody is in charge.

Quality experts claim that up to 75 percent of all quality problems occur as work moves from one department to the next.

Traditional departments are like silos. They're self-contained units, with communication taking place only between the managers at the top (if at all). People in the silos have no way to look out and see what others in the organization are doing.

The highly successful have figured out how to escape the silo mentality.

- They understand how the work they do really takes place and where the problem hand-off points are.

- They identify unnecessary steps that waste time and missing steps that cause errors.

- They see how their work relates to the customer. This helps them know how to set priorities.

- They figure out which other departments, and often which specific people, they need to work smoothly with.

   If you're on a work team of people from several different departments, you're already taking this approach. These cross-functional teams, as they're called, help break down departmental barriers. They bring together the right people needed to get a job done, no matter what departments they come from.

❧ What You Can Do ❧

Even if your organization has not organized around work processes, you can still begin to look at your work horizontally.

   1. Make a list of all of the outputs of your job—information, materials, or services—and who gets each one. For most people in large organizations, these people will be internal customers (other employees within the organization).

   2. Hold conversations with the people who receive your work. Ask them what specifically they need from you. Ask how you could make their jobs easier and more productive. How could the hand-off be easier for them?

3. Next, make a list of the inputs—information, materials, services—you need to do your own job. Beside each input, write down the department (or if possible, the person) it comes from.

4. Hold conversations with the people who provide your inputs. Discuss ways they could make your job easier and more productive. Tell them how you use what you get from them and any problems you've encountered.

5. Talk to your boss to get his or her ideas about taking a horizontal approach to the work of your group.

6. Learn something from each completion. (Note what went well (do it again), what caused stress (how can we fix it), what you forgot this time, and what you wish you'd known when you started.)

7. Be a protector of other departments, not a critic. Do things that make them look good and perform better. Let them know about any problem that's coming their way.

 Tips from the Highly Successful

• **Draw your job.** Your job is much more than the list of duties on a job description. It connects up to other parts of the organization in some very interesting ways. To discover these, make a drawing to illustrate the work steps you perform and how they're related to the work of others. You'll probably see two or three places where you can do some immediate streamlining.

- **Speak plainly.** When talking about your work to people in other departments, use everyday language. Jargon, technical terms, and initials are useful only when everybody understands them. Otherwise, they act as barriers.

- **Do what you can personally to remove barriers between departments.** Be tactful. Don't get defensive when someone offers you an improvement suggestion. In fact, ask for suggestions from others. That opens the door for them to do the same. Learn about the problems and concerns of the groups you work with. If appropriate, cross-train yourself in the tasks other departments perform—or at least become generally familiar with them.

- **Avoid competition with other departments.** Focus on the common goal of satisfying customers.

- **Lose that "it's not my job" attitude.** In today's organizations, everybody needs to be ready to do just about anything. Find ways to pitch in. Don't let things fall through the cracks.

- **Learn the work and the goals of the key departments you work with.** The more you understand what they're up against, the better you'll know what you can do to make their lives easier. Have lunch with people from other departments. Ask them questions about how their group sees your group. What are the specific problems they face? How do they plan to fix them?

- **Pull together.** In the days following a flood, earthquake, or fire, crimes decline and people pull together to take care of each other. Even total strangers help each other. Corporate reengineering, downsizing, rightsizing (or capsizing) demand that same spirit. That feeling of "we're all in it together" is what organizations need today.

Chapter 3

Be a Copy Cat

If you visit the Prado art museum in Spain, you'll see many aspiring artists sitting with easels and canvases in front of renowned paintings. The museum gives them permission to copy these paintings as a way to develop their artistic skills. By copying a great master, they learn the techniques the master used to produce great works of art. They believe there is no better way to learn to become a master painter.

After watching this I thought, "Wouldn't it be wonderful if the original masters could be here to coach these students and show them exactly how they painted their masterpieces and why they did it that way?"

We all know people at work who are very good at what they do—
or some aspect of what they do. Do they owe their ability to some
special inborn gift or talent?

Highly successful people don't think so. Aside from
skills like music and sports, they believe the secret to being an
outstanding performer is simply to learn how to behave like one.
The real challenge, they believe, is finding the best people to
learn from.

In every organization there are people who are outstanding: the most productive salespeople, the most helpful customer
service reps, or the most thorough troubleshooters. Even when
they are not formally recognized by the organization, most people
know who they are.

Then there are people who are particularly good at one
phase of their jobs:

• The engineer who is an expert problem solver.

• The marketing analyst who knows how to "make the data sing."

• The salesperson who excels at getting in to see senior
executives.

• The customer service rep who is especially good at dealing
with irate customers.

• The super-organized person who can efficiently handle a crisis
while completing other tasks as well.

The most successful people seek out these high performers and learn from them. They watch them work, and ask them
to share lessons they've learned. The successful seek to become
a composite of the best.

Finding the Best

It's not always easy to find the best. One secret is to ask several people in your organization to give you the names of the people they think are the best. Then go to your manager and ask the same question. "Who do you consider to be the best people at _____?" Then approach the people who appear on both lists. They're almost certain to be the right people for you to learn from. It's best if you can observe more than one.

❧ What You Can Do ☙

Don't imitate everything another person does, but closely observe high performers and decide which aspects of their work style and practices you'd like to incorporate into your own.

1. Ask to observe several people who demonstrate outstanding performance on the job. Look at their end product. How do their results differ from other people's?

2. Study the steps these people take in producing their end results. See if there are some common elements in what these high performers do.

3. Observe the behavior these people display in getting their work done, in performing the steps of their work. How do these differ from others'?

4. Ask questions of these high performers to determine what information helps them to produce excellent results. What were they thinking about? Do their thought processes differ from those of people who aren't high performers?

5. Seek examples of high performers that appear in newspapers, magazine articles, or case studies. Ponder what they have in common.

6. What do you do exceptionally well? What strengths, skills, or abilities enable you to do this well? How can you apply them to other things you do?

7. If you need help, don't ask someone to do it for you while you walk away or tune out. Ask them to show you how to do it so you can do it yourself next time.

8. Arrange to visit people outside your organization who have a reputation for excellence. Other firms will often let outsiders observe how they operate.

One company's study showed that the most productive salespeople never made cold calls. They did telephone prospecting and got appointments before calling on potential customers.

 Tips from the Highly Successful

• **Don't choose the wrong person to learn from.** There are people whose reputations are undeserved or out of date. Make sure the person you select really has the skills and behaviors you would like to learn. If you're unsure, ask your boss or a co-worker for recommendations.

• **Build shortcuts into the regular work process.** Often old-timers have come up with ingenious ways to improve the process: setting up a piece of equipment, for example, or speeding up a customer order. If it's a good idea, use it—and make sure it gets built into your standard process.

- **Don't limit yourself to people who do your kind of work.** Successful people know they have a lot to learn from any high performer. A customer service person may have a lot to teach you about handling negative feedback, even if you never work directly with customers. A field service technician may have a problem-solving approach you could use in your work as a human resources specialist.

- **Be open to alternative paths to success.** If you're a sales-person who's always made your numbers with a few big sales, try observing a peer who makes more but smaller deals. What can you learn from this person? Watch what other people do rather than having them tell you about it. Research shows that top performers often don't *know* what makes them so effective. Even if they know, they often have a tough time explaining it. Learning to imitate it from their words is nearly impossible.

- **Study your leaders.** Chances are there were some behaviors your leaders displayed that led to their promotion. Carefully observe what they do. How could you adopt (or adapt) some of their best behavior into what you do?

- **Talk through the work process.** If you know people who are good at problem solving or troubleshooting, ask them to talk through their process so you can understand how they came to their conclusions.

- **Talk to yourself out loud.** One highly effective person talks out loud to herself when confronting a tough problem. She finds that saying things aloud makes them clearer. Others listen in and learn from her thought processes as she troubleshoots a complex computer software problem.

Chapter 4

Design Your Own
Cheat Sheets

A group of executives were talking about embarrassing moments when they had forgotten to pack important items for business trips. I told about being in New York for an important speech and rising early in the morning only to discover that I had not packed any neckties. The speech was at 8:00 AM, before any stores would open.

Others told of forgetting to pack belts, dress shoes, and shirts. One woman recalled forgetting her make-up kit and a blouse. Another forgot her shoes. All she had were grubby sneakers she had worn on the plane.

Now I keep a list of all items to be packed for a business trip in a visible place in my closet. A five-second scan of the list prevents embarrassing mistakes.

We all need all the help we can get, especially at work. Highly successful people have figured out how to help themselves by creating their own cheat sheets.

Cheat sheets—or job aids, as they're officially called—are anything that helps you perform a task correctly and quickly. Job aids save time, increase accuracy, and ensure completeness. They also make it easier for others to temporarily take your place when you're away.

One widespread job aid is the recipe. To avoid leaving out a key ingredient, even the best cooks follow a recipe—even if they have cooked the dish hundreds of time.

Checklists are important for tasks with no margin for error, like flying an airplane. They are also useful for important tasks you don't perform often enough to remember from one time to the next.

Audible-izing a Checklist

I went flying with a friend in a small, two-engine plane. He was a former Blue Angel pilot with thousands of hours of flying time.

As he began the process of starting the engine and taxiing onto the runway, he went through a complete checklist, audibly calling out each step, even though I was the only other person in the plane and had no idea what he was talking about. When I asked why he did this, he explained that by following exactly the same routine each time and saying the steps out loud, just as he had done when flying the most complex jet, he could avoid making some small mistake or oversight that could have drastic consequences.

There are many other kinds of job aids:

• Step-by-step diagrams of how to perform a task or assemble a piece of equipment.

• A diagram of how something should look—the setup for tables and chairs at executive briefings, for example, or the layout for food and beverages on a buffet table.

• A calendar for appointments and meetings.

• A recipe, whether it's for making a chocolate cake or mixing chemicals in a giant vat.

• A visible reminder: a "power off?" sign on your computer screen, or a "check enclosed?" note on an envelope.

• An "if . . . then" chart, which includes a series of situations and the appropriate response for each.

• A list of the proper sales tax for various purchase amounts.

• A chart showing which carrier to use to send a package, based on urgency and distance.

• A simple set of instructions on how to do things with your telephone that you do rarely, such as forwarding a message or connecting several people on a conference call.

Create Your Own Job Aid

One person described going to a class to learn new computer software to develop overhead transparencies for presentations. In class, everything seemed clear. But when she returned to her office to begin using the new software, her mind was nearly blank.

Through trial and error, she got somewhat comfortable with the software. Then she wrote down on one sheet of paper the steps necessary to do the basic, frequent tasks for which the software had been designed. Now, when someone asks her to put together a presentation, she has a one-page summary that describes exactly what she needs to do. No more errors, no more panic, and less frustration. How much better the class could have been if it had been organized around the job aid participants would use at their desks.

You probably already create job aids, although you may not think of them in this way. For example, do you always look up phone numbers in the phone book? Don't you have your own list of frequently called numbers? If the list is too long or changes too often, don't you create your own card file?

Highly successful people are always looking for new ways to use job aids. They may compile names and addresses of people who need to receive copies of a report. Or they may list steps to follow in certain emergency situations.

❧ What You Can Do ❧

The widespread, focused use of job aids is in its infancy. Few organizations make extensive job aids available, or encourage people to share the ones they've created on their own.

Take a good look at everything you do. Identify those tasks you do frequently, and see if there are helpful job aids you could create.

1. Draw up a checklist for important tasks you perform on a regular basis. For each task, list the steps. Write down key times or deadlines and the names of those who need to be involved in some way.

2. Create a bulletin board for yourself. Do you have someplace where you can post notes about upcoming events, important reminders, and other items you need to remember? Warning: If your bulletin board gets too crowded, it may be a sign you need to reorganize your work space.

3. Make an "if . . . then" chart. Possible types: responses to typical customer situations; information required for various types of orders; techniques to use at various points in the problem-solving process.

4. Color code. It's easier to find a piece of paper if you know what color you're looking for. If you are involved in many different activities, consider establishing a color code of some kind: blue for one kind of activity, yellow for another (e.g., blue for customers, yellow for suppliers, green for home office correspondence), and so forth. Then be sure to use paper, ink, folders, and/or labels of the right color for the right activity.

5. Keep a calendar and/or time organizer. These are often in notebook form, with places to keep phone numbers, expense receipts, and lists of things to do. Or they may be electronic organizers or small computers known as PDAs (personal digital assistants) that fit in your pocket or briefcase.

6. Compile your own phone list or card file. Make sure it is easily accessible. Even if you know all the important numbers, someone filling in for you probably won't.

7. Compare your job aids with those of your co-workers. Any ideas worth sharing? If you've devised a job aid that works for you, it will probably work for others.

8. Create an index for your filing system. That will speed up the process of finding things.

9. Create a form that shows all the information you'll need to fill a request: what the person needs, how soon, the budget code, and where to send it. This eliminates a follow-up call to get missing information.

10. Keep a record of items you frequently order for your work, complete with stock number and description. The list may be only 10 items long, but it will speed up the reorder process.

 Tips from the Highly Successful

• **Don't overlook your computer:** If you have one, it can be the ultimate job aid. Computers can help organize almost every aspect of your working and personal life, from writing checks to scheduling appointments, from tracking your to-do list to routing documents. Are you using your organization's computer system for this purpose? Who are the people—in information services, perhaps—who could help you take better advantage of your computer?

- **Make it easy for people to substitute for you if necessary.**
Successful people realize they need to make it easy for others to
step in and take over for them on occasion. They keep checklists
and other job aids on hand for others to use: lists of people and
how they can help, phone numbers, and even a list of places to
eat lunch.

- **Create a paper trail.** To avoid scrambling for a solution to a
problem you've solved in the past, keep a list of solutions you've
tried, noting what worked and what didn't. The next time something similar happens, review what you did about it last time.

- **Be your own secretary.** Remember when secretaries kept
their bosses organized and on track? Those days are gone forever.
It's up to you to keep yourself organized.

- **Revisit your cheat sheets.** Things change. Procedures get
altered. Keep job aids current.

Chapter 5

Speed Thrills

I was visiting a large automobile production plant in Europe. The plant was about 10 years old, but the housekeeping was spotless. You really could eat off the floors. But the workers were proudest of the speed with which they changed the enormous dies that stamped out fenders and door panels. Where once it had taken three to four hours to change one die, they were now doing it in 10 to 12 minutes. Their target was three minutes. Dramatically shrinking the time for this complex task gave the entire plant great pride. They beamed when they talked about it, and that success led them to reduce the time for many other jobs in the plant.

Where I live, going to the post office can be a frustrating experience. The lines are often long, but we all encounter long lines in other places. What's maddening about this post office is the pace of the workers. It's like watching a slow-motion film of people working. And you can be standing in line near lunchtime, only to have the window slammed shut when the lunch hour arrives.

Contrast that with the people who deliver air parcels. They're often dressed in shorts, presumably making it easier and cooler for them to run. And run they do.

Which two of the following three attributes are most important to an organization's success? (Hint: This is a trick question.)

Better
Faster
Cheaper

To be successful in today's competitive world, you've got to be better, faster, *and* cheaper. But don't worry. Faster is nearly always cheaper, and need not cut into better, either—if your work processes are efficient and effective and you have a personal desire to be as productive as possible. Reducing the time it takes to do things applies to everything that happens inside the organization. You can shave time off:

- Collecting overdue accounts receivable.

- Preparing the annual budget.

- Processing orders.

- Preparing monthly financial statements.

- Inserting a part in a subassembly.

- Developing the next-generation product.

- Doing the monthly close in accounting.

In fact, everything we do is a candidate for cycle time reduction.

Did you ever notice how much you can accomplish when you're pushing against a deadline? And how satisfying it is to get so much done in such a short period of time? Like riding down a hill on your bike, working fast can be exhilarating. And productive.

No one wants to work at a killer pace for too long—or work so fast that details are overlooked and quality suffers. Still, highly successful people know there's a lot to be said for working fast.

- They get a lot of personal satisfaction from performing a task quickly and from moving along from task to task without wasting time. It's a turn-on to feel on top of things.

- They make co-workers more productive by responding quickly to their questions and requests.

- They know that getting something done for a customer on time or early is one of the best ways to keep—and increase—that customer's business.

&⊗ What You Can Do ⊗&

It is difficult to force another person to work faster. It's got to be something you try out on your own. Highly successful people view working faster as a personal challenge and respond accordingly.

One subtle reason people work slowly is that they realize there isn't enough work to keep them busy. They slow down to make the work they have fill the time available. Don't fall into that trap. Instead, go find more work to do. Ask others who are swamped how you can help them. Go to your leader and ask for additional tasks.

1. Just for fun, try shaving a few minutes from a task you perform frequently. For example, if it normally takes you 10 minutes to write up a sales call, try doing it in eight. Then ask yourself if anything suffered as a result of doing it faster. Were there any gains? Reward the calculating person in you.

2. Promise yourself you will always return calls within a certain period of time—at least by the end of the day, sooner if possible. Notice how good it feels not to have to apologize for not calling back sooner.

3. Talk to the people in other departments you work with. What keeps the work from moving more rapidly from one stage to the next? What can you do about it?

4. Batch tasks. Do similar tasks—those that require the same materials or involve talking to the same people, for example—at the same time.

5. Handle paperwork once. Don't put that piece of paper in your "I'll finish it later" pile. Do your part and move it on.

6. Get into the habit of doing things now rather than putting them off. That guarantees a quicker pace.

7. Do the small, quick tasks first and get them off your plate. Sometimes the sheer size of your to-do list delays your getting started while you try to figure

out what to do first. But get started on the most important tasks facing you, not just the most urgent.

8. Schedule your day with your personal energy cycle in mind. If you're a morning person, schedule your toughest (and most important) activities early.

 Tips from the Highly Successful

• **Vary your pace.** No one can work flat-out forever. So vary the pace of your day. For some activities, especially those that are new to you, you need to work more slowly and carefully. For others, you can work fast.

• **Think BIG.** Individual improvements can eventually add up to major savings in time, especially when technology is added to the mix. Many banks and insurance companies, for example, have reduced the time it takes to process applications from weeks to mere hours. You probably can't manage such improvements on your own, but they can give you some idea of what is possible.

• **Do more things at the same time.** In an assembly-line mentality, we used to work on a project in a series of steps, with each group waiting until the previous group had done its work. Now with computer technology and the right planning, many groups can work on different parts of a project simultaneously, bringing it all together only in the final steps.

• **Take breaks to recharge your energy.** Don't skip lunch every day. You can't work at top speed all day without some break. Take time to recharge.

• **Accelerate parts of a project.** When you're overwhelmed, try negotiating some tasks down or into smaller pieces. "I can't get the whole thing to you tomorrow, but I can get the first half tomorrow and the rest the next day."

Chapter 6

Don't Just Do It.
Do It Better!

I was at a track meet in the Stanford stadium when the announcer said over the microphone, "The runners are on a pace that could break the world record." Nearly everyone rose off their seats. Few people can resist feeling a rush of adrenaline at such a moment.

Even if you're thousands of miles away watching the Olympic slalom race on television, and at the bottom of the screen you see the skier's time compared to the world record, witnessing a new record being set is always a thrill. Someone has just done something faster or better than anyone ever did before.

There's a story about a company doing a reference check on a potential new employee. The human resources person asks the former employer, "Was Harold a steady worker?"

"Steady?" the former employer said. "He was more than steady. He was motionless."

Twenty years ago, being described as a steady worker would have been the highest compliment. No longer. To succeed in today's organization requires far more. The organization expects you to do the best you can all the time. But beyond that, it expects you to constantly get better. That requires putting out extra effort.

The best athletes stand out not just because of their athletic ability, but because they go all out, scramble after every ball, and try to make every play. (If they don't, they're likely to get booed.)

Great stage performers hold nothing back. Sit close enough, and you'll see the effort they're expending as perspiration drips down their faces and soaks their clothes.

The same is true for highly successful people on the job. They're distinguished not only by what they know and what they do, but by the extra effort they're willing to put into their work.

They know they weren't hired just to do their jobs. They were hired to constantly do their jobs *better.* And they've discovered that there is no limit to the improvements that can be made. Some people think it's impossible to keep getting better, but they're flat-out wrong.

Every organization worth its salt today sponsors improvement efforts to boost efficiency and to be more responsive to customers. You may already be involved in one or more of these broad improvement activities.

But even working strictly on your own, you can always find ways to make your own improvements. Roger Milliken, CEO of the Milliken Corporation, said, "We have learned that 80 percent of the breakthroughs have come from people who are actually working on the machines and computers on the plant floor or office."

When the American Productivity Center surveyed companies to find out where they got their ideas for productivity improvement, 62 percent of the companies identified employee ideas as the most important source. Management-initiated changes were chosen by only 2.5 percent of the companies as the most important source of productivity improvement. You are the best source of improved performance.

The problem is, we get so used to our daily routine that we may no longer notice things that need improving. It's a little like not noticing your carpet needs cleaning until your relatives come to visit.

To take a fresh look at our jobs, we may need to adopt an outsider's point of view. Imagine that somebody showed you a videotape of you doing your job. After you finished apologizing for your appearance (which is what most people first do when they see themselves on video), you might see things you'd never noticed before:

• How long you have to search through materials to find what you need.

• The fact that your equipment and materials are not conveniently placed.

• The number of times you get interrupted.

• The relatively small amount of time you spend on your assigned tasks.

Successful people know how to step back occasionally and look at their jobs as if they were outsiders—not to criticize their own performance, but to find ways of doing their jobs better. Once you start looking, you'll find lots of improvement opportunities, especially if you can leave behind the attitude of "that's the way we do it because that's the way we've always done it."

If you were the owner of your company, wouldn't you look for, retain, and promote those people who relentlessly made things better, in contrast to those who were merely steady workers?

Take initiative.[1] Many people in organizations turn in a suggestion or write a memo to someone in management calling attention to some problem or opportunity. And they think they're taking initiative. They're wrong.

That's the minimum the organization expects from everyone. People who display true initiative go way beyond that. They're not content to turn in an idea or pass a suggestion up the line. They plunge in and make sure their ideas get implemented. They keep pushing until things get better.

Working Smarter

A man and wife were chopping wood. The man worked all day and stopped only once for a quick lunch. The wife took numerous breaks throughout the day and even enjoyed a quick nap after lunch. At the end of the day, the man was upset to find that his wife had chopped as much wood as he had. "I simply don't understand it," he said. "Every time I looked up, there you were sitting down." She replied, "Well, I guess you didn't notice. Every time I sat down, I sharpened my ax."

---

1. This is one of the Basic Principles that form the basis of all Zenger Miller programs. See Appendix 1.

๑๛ **What You Can Do** ๛๑

In today's competitive world, no improvement that increases efficiency or customer satisfaction is too small. Before you make changes you'll want to check with your boss and others who might be affected, but don't let that stop you from looking around and getting some ideas now.

1. Review your personal performance numbers. When you measured your work as suggested in Chapter 1, what improvement opportunities turned up? Did some tasks take longer than you thought? Were there things you did that seemed inefficient?

2. Take a look at how your work space is organized. Chances are you never took the time to set things up for maximum efficiency. Are the "tools" of your job efficiently organized? Are your files where you need them? Do you have instant access to information you use all the time, such as phone numbers or order codes?

3. Question procedures. The last thing you want to do is rush off and rewrite procedures you don't like. But that doesn't mean you can't question them. Find out why you need three signatures for that requisition, for example. Maybe there's a good reason. On the other hand, maybe it's a holdover and no longer necessary.

4. Make a video. If you have access to a video camera and can set it up without too much trouble, why not put it on a tripod and tape yourself working at intervals throughout an average day? The results may surprise you.

If making a video isn't realistic, get a fresh perspective by asking a friend to take a look at your work area. Or compare yours with the work areas of people who do work similar to yours.

5. Double-check your work. If you're putting a big order together or working on a major project, double-check to make sure everything is on schedule and there will be no delays or errors.

6. Post your charts in a place where you and others can see the progress you are making.

7. Get a coach. Top tennis players hire a coach to help them get better. Maybe they just won Wimbledon or the U.S. Open. They're already the best in the world. But they hire a coach to help them get better—to overcome bad habits and not let sloppy practices creep in.

8. Chunk. Tackle a part of your work life, not the whole thing at once.

 Tips from the Highly Successful

• **Don't invite burnout.** "Doing things better" means over the long haul, not just in the short term. Don't work yourself into the ground. Find ways to work smarter.

• **Maintain your focus.** Any improvements should increase customer satisfaction or promote efficiency, either directly or indirectly. Reducing the time it takes to answer customer requests is definitely on target. Buying expensive equipment may not be. If you're not sure about an improvement, talk it over with your boss or co-workers. If you need to, find a way to quantify its impact. What is the payoff for that new equipment to you? To others? How can you prove it?

• **Read/talk/listen.** Improvement is in the air these days. Everywhere you turn, people are discussing ways to become more competitive. Keep your eyes open for magazine and newspaper articles, books, and group events where you can share and learn.

• **Be a coach.** When you become experienced and highly effective, one of the best ways to continue your growth, and to pay back what you received, is to be a coach for others.

Chapter 7

Trim Your Waste

I have a friend who is an executive in a large savings and loan. He wanted to become more familiar with the information services department, so he volunteered to go work there for a day. He showed up dressed casually and said, "Here I am, put me to work. Treat me like a new employee." So the supervisor told him they needed to run four reports and gave him precise instructions on how to produce these lengthy computer runs.

They came spitting out of the high-speed printers and he proudly came into her office weighed down with the four reports. She said, "OK, tear off the edges of reports 1, 2, and 4. Throw the third report away, because management doesn't read that one." He could barely contain his frustration when the supervisor said, "That's how management wants it to be done, and that's how we've always done it around here."

William Conway, one of the early leaders of the total quality movement, wrote: "The level of waste in American industry runs between 20 percent and 50 percent of net sales, averaging around 35 percent." (*The Quality and Productivity Equation,* edited by Ross Robson, Productivity Press, Cambridge, Mass., 1990, p. 125.)

But the financial health of every organization depends in part on how the people inside use its resources. While estimates vary widely, organizations that have rigorously studied their overall cost structure discovered that approximately 40 percent of their costs were unnecessary. This "cost of quality" represented the rework and inefficiency in their systems.

Thousands of little deeds begin to add up. For example:

• Throwing away expensive printed brochures rather than putting them back into stock.

• Making unnecessary long-distance telephone calls.

• Shipping packages overnight when regular delivery is in plenty of time.

• Leaving computer monitors running all night and over the weekend, consuming power needlessly.

• Eating expensive meals while traveling.

• Using company letterhead as scratch paper.

• Letting a machine drift out of alignment to produce faulty parts.

• Filing documents that will never be used.

• Not getting the best fares for travel.

What are the conse-
quences of waste? It is an anchor
halting productivity. It slows the
organization down like barnacles
on a ship's hull.

> **Q: What is waste?**
> **A: Anything that adds**
> **to cost and does not**
> **add value.**

If you are in a competitive
industry (and who isn't these days), waste allows new competitors to spring to life. Waste creates the opportunity for them to
succeed. If they operate efficiently and your company is wasteful, you've just invited them to come in and "eat your lunch."

> **The most wasted**
> **resource in most**
> **organizations is time.**

While it can be quite
costly to waste tangible things,
the biggest waste in most organizations is time. It happens in
several ways.

• People work on make-work activities or projects, like the
soldier who is commanded to dig a hole and then fill it in. Some
of the things people do just don't make any difference. Running
a report that gets thrown away is a good example.

• People work on a project of minor value while something
of real importance is being ignored. The maintenance crew is
rearranging the furniture in the cafeteria when they should be
fixing a broken machine on the production floor.

• People work unproductively on valuable activities. They're
stuck in unfocused meetings with people who needn't be
involved.

• People perform some task that is required by policy or to
please some higher-level manager but that adds no value to the
firm's product or service and doesn't serve the customer. Multiple approvals on a requisition are an example.

• People repeat a task because it was not done properly the first time. Anything done for the second time because of an error or omission is wasteful. It has been estimated that one-fourth of all workers don't produce anything, they just fix others' mistakes.

• People take longer on a task because they're looking for the right paper or the right tool. If things are so disorganized that it takes extra time to sort through all of the papers, or search through the files, or rummage through the tool bin, that's classic waste.

• People work on the wrong project because someone forgot to tell them the specifications changed or the customers changed their minds.

• People don't work at all. Anyone who is reading a magazine for pleasure or playing a computer game during working hours is being wasteful.

In most organizations, the costs associated with people are the largest expense, often more than half of the total expenditures of the firm. Assuming the company has a 5 percent return on sales, increasing productivity by only 5 percent would increase profits by 50 percent! A 10 percent increase in productivity would double profits.

Spend a Little to Save a Lot

One large appliance company found a way to spend a little money, but save a great deal more. When its delivery people left the warehouse with an appliance to deliver, they called the customer from a cellular phone in the truck to make sure someone would be there to receive the delivery. If they couldn't reach the customer, they called a neighbor whose name they had requested.

Or they called the customer at work. They wanted to avoid arriving at their destination and finding no one home, wasting their time and tying up an expensive delivery truck in non-productive work.

❦ What You Can Do ❧

Personally crusade against waste. Start with what you directly control or influence. Move out to activities around you, looking for anything that squanders money, time, or materials.

1. Get your work space well organized. Whether it's your car, a desk, a cubicle, or a space on a production line, make it orderly.

2. Spend time doing worthwhile tasks. Make sure you are working on something that adds value.

3. Stay busy all the time. If you run out of work, ask around for something you can do.

4. Don't waste other people's time. Don't go into their work spaces and engage them in long conversations that have no real purpose. That is wasteful of both your time and theirs.

5. Don't allow others to waste your time.

6. Streamline directions for a task you are asked to accomplish. Make a timeline or a simple list of what you need to know or do to get the job done.

7. Share expensive equipment with other groups.

8. Check into less expensive means to get something done. Look for the lowest-cost way to do

something while still satisfying the customer or meeting the real need. If it is only a few pages, fax it. Use regular mail if you have time, or two-day priority instead of overnight express.

9. Negotiate down. If customers ask you to fax them a large document, ask what they specifically need. Would a part of the document be satisfactory? If they ask for a delivery tomorrow, find out if a delivery late in the day is OK. Sometimes people ask for things early because they don't know if they can trust you to deliver when you say you will. Find out when they really need the item.

Volunteering

An administrative assistant in a bank tells of seeing the company interview temporary employees to assist another department on a word processing project. She was not particularly busy, so she asked for information about the project, determined she could fit it into her schedule, and volunteered to take it on. Everyone won. The bank saved the expense of an extra employee. The administrative assistant kept busy and productive and felt better about herself. And a bond of goodwill was created between two departments.

Tips from the Highly Successful

• **Keep your work space clean and neat.** In addition to it looking better, well-organized work spaces are more efficient.

• **Use company resources as if they were your own.** Spend company money as frugally as if it were coming out of your own pocket. Care for equipment and furniture as if it belonged to you.

• **Keep personal business to a minimum during the work day.** Sure, there will always be the occasion when you have to handle some personal issue during the work day, but try to restrict it to emergencies.

• **Behave as if you were the owner of the firm you work for.** If the company is doing wasteful things, speak up. That's what owners do.

PART TWO

HOW TO WORK EFFECTIVELY IN TODAY'S BOUNDARYLESS ORGANIZATION

Highly successful employees make it a point to know the big picture and how they fit in. They probe to find out where the organization is headed. They keep track of the trends that will affect its future—trends concerning customers, the competition, the economy, and emerging new technology. They find out what their organization looks like to the outside world—especially to the customers and suppliers who deal with it.

Narrow defined jobs and traditional lines of authority are fading. Employees today are working in all kinds of formal and informal groups, both permanent and temporary. In these groups everyone works together to solve problems, make decisions, handle their own disagreements, and help each other get the job done.

This new organization requires a culture of cooperation, not competition. A willingness to communicate is the rule, and people genuinely look out for each other.

Chapter 8

Decode Your Mission and Vision Statements

Not long after we founded Zenger Miller came the rise of interest in Japanese management practices. One of the most intriguing ideas we read described how the newest employees at Matsushita would stand up in front of their co-workers and describe their understanding of the mission, vision, and values of the company. That felt right.

Getting our executives to put on paper why the organization existed was powerful. Making explicit the things we believed in seemed like a step that would help recruit the right people. The discipline of writing down a vision of the future is the essence of any long-range planning process. What better way could there be to develop the culture of a new company than to share these views with everyone, and encourage their discussion?

We called all of this our philosophy statement and printed it on a small accordion-folded piece of paper that everyone could keep in a wallet, a purse, or a business card case. Of all the steps we took in our early years, that was at the top. We found that an organization that openly stated its values drew the best people like a magnet. Our philosophy statement became our best recruiting tool.

We printed this philosophy statement on $8\frac{1}{2}$" x 11" pages and gave them to our associates. People framed them and hung them at their work stations. The document helped build a uniform culture. If anyone, including the CEO, behaved in a manner contrary to what it stated, they got called on it. Rightly so. Anyone who believed it had been violated spoke up.

The influence of the vision, mission, and values statement turned out to be even greater on executives than on others. Unfortunately, many of the early professors and practitioners in the training and development field said one thing but back home did just the opposite. We vowed that we would not be two-faced and that we'd "practice what we teach." Having our beliefs and our vision in writing constantly held our feet to the fire. (For a copy of the original Zenger Miller philosophy statement, see Appendix 2.)

There's a story that humorously illustrates what happens when you don't do this.

The New Employee

A young man went to work for a cement-pipe manufacturing company. His first day on the job, he spent his lunch hour wandering about, looking at this strange new environment.

As he walked into the shipping department he looked in awe at the enormous stacks of pipes of all sizes. Huge cranes were motionless because it was the lunch hour. Then the phone rang. No one was around, but it kept ringing and ringing. So the young man went over and answered it.

On the line was an extremely irate customer. "Where in the blankety-blank is my order? My name is Arnold Furster and my construction company has come to a complete halt until we get your pipe."

"I don't know," stammered the young man.

"Well, when will the order be shipped?" the customer bellowed.

"I don't know that either."

"Is the order even in production now?" The customer was now screaming as loud as he could.

"I don't know the answer to that."

"Well, what exactly do you know?" the customer shouted.

"When I answered the phone and said 'Hello,' I told you all I know about the company," the young man replied.

Unfortunately, there are real people like this in many organizations. They don't understand what the company is about, its products, or its clients. Worse yet, they don't understand what the organization stands for, why it exists, what it believes in, or what course it is on. And they aren't even aware that lacking such information greatly hampers their contribution to the organization.

A mission statement describes the reasons why the organization exists. A vision statement describes where the organization wants to be in the future. These are often accompanied by a statement describing the values of the organization, or the principles it holds highest and the code of conduct that springs from that. Sometimes, as in the early days of Zenger Miller, these are combined into one philosophy statement. But whatever form they take, such documents help you understand what your organization is all about and how you can best contribute. They usually start something like this:

"As a company we are dedicated to . . ."

"Our vision is to be the most/biggest/best . . ."

"The values for which we stand are . . ."

"We exist to . . ."

An organization's mission and vision statements are the best windows into the thinking of executives about why the organization exists and where it is going. These are serious documents. This is especially true for organizations that have reorganized or reengineered and need to clarify their new direction. In fact, in today's organization the mission statement may be the only steady beacon in a dark and stormy sea of change.

It's true that mission statements often contain generalities. But successful people know how to look deeper and find the good stuff: *where the organization is headed, what it values most, and especially what kinds of behavior will be rewarded along the way.* They can then make sure that their own priorities and efforts are in sync.

What does your organization's mission statement say?

• If it features phrases like "providing cutting-edge solutions" or "leading the industry" in new technology, then employees' creative, problem-solving abilities and technical skills may be well rewarded—more, perhaps, than people skills.

• If it emphasizes outstanding customer service, then "nice" employees who create satisfied customers will probably be valued.

• If the mission statement dwells on being a low-cost provider through operational efficiency, then well-organized, systematic behavior will probably get more recognition.

☙ What You Can Do ❧

To figure out what your mission statement and vision statement really mean, you may have to do some digging. Make an extra effort to see how they relate to the work *you* do.

1. Keep your organization's mission and vision statement where you'll see them often. Discuss them with your colleagues and your boss. Reread them until you know them well enough to explain them in your own words to another person.

2. Look at the words in your mission and vision statements. How many refer to customers? Employees? Financial success? Outstanding products or services? This very unscientific analysis may tell you something about where your organization wants you to put your energies. Note what comes first. It's often a clue about what your management values most.

3. List your major tasks or responsibilities. Ask yourself how they support the directions and goals outlined in the mission and vision statements. Do you see how your job ties into the mission of the organization? How could you bring it into closer alignment? Is the vision clear to you?

4. Write your own personal mission statement, taking off from your organization's version. (If you're on a team, you may already have created such a document.) See if your leader has any suggestions for what you've written.

5. Pay attention to what your executives say in public meetings or to the press about your company's mission and vision of the future.

6. Read company literature to absorb the information and language of your organization. Your communication style needs to be in sync with the organization's.

Here are three sample vision statements. Notice how each communicates a sense of the culture of the company. Don't you get some idea of what it would be like to work for them?

Honda

HONDA MOTOR CO., LTD.
Company Principle

"Maintaining an international viewpoint, we are dedicated to supplying products of the highest efficiency yet at a reasonable price for worldwide customer satisfaction."

HONDA MOTOR CO., LTD.
Management Policy

- ❏ Proceed always with ambition and youthfulness.
- ❏ Respect sound theory, develop fresh ideas, and make the most effective use of time.
- ❏ Enjoy your work, and always brighten your working atmosphere.
- ❏ Strive constantly for a harmonious flow of work.
- ❏ Be ever mindful of the value of research and endeavor.

HONDA OF AMERICA MFG., INC.
Operating Priorities

In all areas of manufacturing operations, Honda of America Manufacturing, Inc. observes the following priorities:

1. Safety
2. Quality
3. Production

HONDA OF AMERICA MFG., INC.
Operating Principles

Quality In All Jobs
Learn, Think, Analyze, Evaluate, and Improve

Reliable Products
On Time, with Excellence, and Consistency

Better Communication
Listen, Ask, and Speak Up

1995 SLOGAN
"One Team Building Our Future"

Source: Honda Motor Co., Ltd. Used with permission.

Ben & Jerry's

Ben & Jerry's is dedicated to the creation and demonstration of a new corporate concept of linked prosperity. Our mission consists of three interrelated parts:

PRODUCT MISSION: To make, distribute, and sell the finest quality, all-natural ice cream and related products in a wide variety of innovative flavors made from Vermont dairy products.

SOCIAL MISSION: To operate the company in a way that actively recognizes the central role that business plays in the structure of society by initiating ways to improve the quality of life of a broad community—local, national, and international.

ECONOMIC MISSION: To operate the company on a sound financial basis of profitable growth, increasing value for our shareholders, and creating career opportunities and financial rewards for our employees.

Underlying the mission of Ben & Jerry's is the determination to seek new and creative ways of addressing all three parts, while holding a deep respect for the individuals, inside and outside the company, and for the communities of which they are a part.

Source: Ben & Jerry's. Used with permission.

Steelcase

OLD MISSION STATEMENT
Our mission is to provide
the world's best office environment
products, services, systems, and intelligence . . .
designed to help people in offices
work more effectively.

NEW MISSION STATEMENT
Helping people work more effectively.

Source: Steelcase. Used with permission.

Tips from the Highly Successful

• **See if you can find out what was *not* included.** A mission, vision, or values statement can seem bland. But behind every smoothly worded phrase there were probably hours of heated discussion and maybe even a fight or two. That's because they are not so much written as hammered out in a series of meetings—word by word, comma by comma, sentence by sentence. Find out who was involved in writing the document. Ask them about the issues people struggled with. When you find out what was *not* included, you'll know more about the importance of what *was*.

• **Compare the new with the old.** If your organization has recently adopted a new mission statement, see if you can find a copy of the old one. A comparison of the differences will tell you which direction and values are most important now.

• **Don't pooh-pooh the "vision thing."** Two Stanford University business professors chose 1926 to retroactively invest one imaginary dollar in each of 20 companies that were most often described as "visionary." By 1990 that one dollar had grown to $6,356—as compared to only $955 for a dollar invested in non-visionary direct competitors. To learn more about the impact of vision on corporate success, read *Built to Last: Successful Habits of Visionary Companies,* by James C. Collins and Jerry I. Porras. (Harper Business, Div. of Harper Collins. NY, NY.)

• **If you suspect you don't fit in, take action.** When you take your mission statement seriously, you can't help but sense to what extent you fit in with its directions and values. You'll never be successful if your values don't fit. The organization will reject you like the human body rejects foreign tissue that doesn't match. Successful people who suspect they're out of sync take action. They discuss their concerns with colleagues and with their boss.

They may try to change the system from within. Or they may decide it's time to think about moving on. If the values and vision of your organization are not ones you can fully support, then you are probably in the wrong organization. Talk with the leaders of your company to find out if you belong or if you should look for a place to work that fits you better.

Chapter 9

Think Like Your
Own Customer

I purchased a new automobile, and when I took it in for its 30,000-mile checkup the service manager asked if there were any problems with it. I explained that my niece had tried to put in a cassette tape when there was already one inside, which had jammed inside the radio/tape-deck unit.

The service manager said, "Well, we can't have you driving around without a working tape player. We'll order a new unit for you and if you'll come in any day next week, we can get it installed in about one hour."

So I took the car in. When I picked it up and drove out, I turned the radio on. "Drat," I thought, "I'm going to have to program all six AM stations and the 12 FM stations I programmed in before." I turned the radio on and hit the first button. To my utter amazement, every button was programmed just like my old radio had been.

Two days later, the tape that had been jammed in the old tape deck arrived in the mail, accompanied by a note apologizing for having forgotten to give it to me.

This is a classic case of an organization putting itself in the customer's shoes.

Thinking like a customer should come naturally to all of us. We spend hours as customers—shopping, pricing, ordering, using, enjoying, breaking, fixing, complaining, fuming, and reordering.

The trick is to think like your *own* customer. Highly successful people bring a customer mindset to work. While they're working, they're also asking themselves, "Is what I'm doing going to make a positive difference for my customer?"

Such thinking comes naturally to people who deal directly with the ultimate customers. But even if you never see customers in your work—if you're a financial analyst, say, or a purchasing agent—you should still be able to demonstrate that what you do benefits your customers.

Successful people have learned two important secrets that help them think like customers.

• Number one, customers are self-centered. Maybe someone in another department lost their order. Maybe your phone system is inefficient. Maybe it does take five days to get an application from the mailroom to your desk.

Guess what? Your customers don't care. They want the products they ordered. They want to reach the right person with one phone call. They want their application approved now. If your organization can't meet these requirements—which are, after all, pretty basic—your customers will find other organizations that can.

• Number two, customers have their own concerns. They are happy when you understand these concerns and know how your products or services can help meet them. They are ecstatic when you anticipate their concerns—and come up with solutions they never dreamed were possible.

ᏬᏬ What You Can Do ᏬᏬ

The more you think like a customer, the more you'll help your organization keep its old customers and get new ones. If you're a salesperson or a customer service rep, you deal directly with customers and probably already know how to think like one. But if you work in another job, there are things you can do to get inside your customer's skin.

1. Think about the last few times you were a customer. What did you like about these transactions? What didn't you like? What lessons could you apply to your own job?

2. Depending on your position, you may not know much about the end product or service your organization provides. Take time to find out. Read marketing materials. Stay current with magazine and newspaper articles on your industry. Talk to employees who are directly involved with the ultimate customer. See what the issues are from a customer's point of view.

3. Observe how customers actually use your product or service. Talk with people who use it. Go watch it in use. If yours is a service company, see the service being performed. Find out why some potential customers aren't using your company's products, and then help to change that.

4. Go out of your way to support people who work directly with customers. As far as the customers are concerned, these employees *are* the company.

5. Achieve harmony with your customer. The most successful people have learned to get into sync with their customers in their volume, pace, and tone of voice. The more you act and sound like them, the more influential you'll be. (But don't respond to rudeness with more rudeness, and never be phony).

6. Start off on the right foot. Customers are especially sensitive to little things that happen at the beginning of the relationship. They think, "Does this slight oversight signal that your organization is sloppy and doesn't care? Is it the tip of a giant iceberg or a random error?" Work especially hard at the beginning to be perfect in your relationship with a new client.

One of the founders of Apple Computer, Steve Wozniak, worked weekends in a retail computer store. What better way to understand how potential customers thought and what they needed from a personal computer?

 Tips from the Highly Successful

• **Don't be put off by complicated products or services.**
Even if your organization produces highly technical products or services, you can understand how they work. Start with articles about your organization's product or service written by your company. Also look for articles in general-interest magazines and newspapers, which explain concepts in terms the average person can understand. Talk with people who can explain the products to you.

• **There's a difference between an internal and an external customer.** If you've participated in TQM or other improvement efforts, you've heard about "internal customers"—the people in your organization who use your output to produce their output. It's important to meet their needs. But to truly understand the big picture and how you fit into it, you have to learn how to think like an external customer.

• **Keep customers informed.** Let customers know what you need from them. Be sure you know what deadlines must be met. If you can't meet a deadline, suggest alternatives that will produce the same result. A periodic fax or postcard to let the customers know their order is progressing on schedule is a powerful signal that you care.

If you get a request in writing, confirm that you've received it and that you'll deliver on time. If it looks as though there will be a delay, immediately let your customer know.

• **Survey your customers.** The only way you know for sure that you're serving customers better is to make a baseline measure. That yardstick lets you know if you're improving, standing still, or sliding backwards. The survey doesn't need to be long or complicated. Make up a series of question that focus on what you do for your customers (internal or external) and give people a scale on which to answer. For example:

How satisfied are you with how promptly I provide information you request?

1	2	3	4	5	6	7	8	9	10
Very Unsatisfied							Totally Satisfied		

Chapter 10

Create Brief Encounters
of the Productive Kind

I worked with an executive in a pharmaceutical company who maintained a challenging schedule. In addition to being the head of research for this multinational firm, he was a full-time professor at Stanford University. He would often schedule 5- or 10-minute meetings. Initially, people were resentful of such brief business meetings. They were more accustomed to the one-half-hour to hour-long meetings that most secretaries automatically schedule. But you found yourself being on time and passing by much of the unnecessary small talk to get right to the heart of the matter in your meetings with him. It was amazing what you could get done if you went in expecting the meeting to be short. While some things got missed in a short meeting, he was able to conduct five or six times as many meetings as his colleagues. (If you needed more time and pushed for it, you could schedule longer appointments.)

As organizations get flatter and leaner, most of us find we're dealing with many more people than we used to, often from many more parts of the organization.

Highly successful people know how valuable these interactions are, and how much they can accomplish in them. They also know the value of these encounters is not determined by their length. In fact, given the number of our interactions in any given day, there's a definite advantage to making them short and sweet.

The trick is to be able to turn even a casual conversation into a productive exchange if you need to—one that can help reach a goal, improve a situation, or make a working relationship stronger.

Here are some interactions that qualify as productive exchanges. Check off any you've experienced recently.

• Solving a problem for an unhappy customer.

• Convincing a co-worker to help on a project.

• Resolving a conflict in your group.

• Giving feedback to someone about his or her performance.

• Receiving feedback about your own performance.

• Gathering important information from another department or work group.

• Passing on an improvement suggestion.

• Assessing how a co-worker really feels about a project.

Many people avoid exchanges like these, for fear they will be too difficult and take too long. Highly successful people don't shy away, because they've learned the secret of handling them effectively and relatively quickly. They're skilled at cutting to the heart of the matter as efficiently as possible.

There are two distinct kinds of interactions. One is the kind you initiate and control to some degree. The second occurs when you're on the receiving end.

Outstanding athletes will often strategize or play out an upcoming game in their minds. You can do the same thing for important or difficult interactions on the job.

Handling Brief Interactions You Initiate

The secret comes down to a process of *mental rehearsal.*

Successful people think about the situation, plan what they want to say and do, and then play out a conversation in their heads. They imagine how the other person will respond and adapt their remarks accordingly. They'll play out two or three different scenes, knowing they can't totally predict what the other person will say or how he or she will react.

For example, if you need help from someone on a project, you might go through the following mental process: (Note: you are playing both parts of the conversation.)

You: "Mary, we really need your help on this project, because you're the only person with the experience to be able to pull it off in the time we've got."

You guess what Mary will say: "Sorry, I'm too swamped with other assignments," or "Well, I'll do it if you can get me some relief from my other assignments," or "Yes, I'd like to but I can't get started for at least two weeks." Obviously, each of these calls for a different response. But, it pays to have thought through the likely alternatives and what you would say to each. While Mary's actual response won't be exactly like any of the ones you've mentally rehearsed, chances are one will be close.

The key is to actually say in your mind the words you'll say to Mary. Don't be general or describe your approach to the conversation. (For example, don't say, "I'll talk with Mary and get her reaction to working on this project, and I'll answer any concerns she has." That's far too vague and gets you nowhere.) Actually say it—word by word—so you can rehearse the exact phrases and sentences you'll use. When you do that, you'll find that some ways of saying it don't come off all that well, and you'll modify them. Other phrases you'll find comfortable and will lock in for future replay. This seemingly simple process is extremely powerful in making brief interactions work well.

In most cases, mental rehearsal is enough. For sensitive situations, you may want to actually practice with someone, after giving him or her some background on how the other person might respond. That someone could be a work associate, someone in human resources, your spouse, or a close friend.

Handling Brief Interactions You Don't Initiate

We joke about some people being clueless. They are in discussions but miss the point. They walk through situations and, like the nearsighted Mr. Magoo, fail to see danger or opportunity.

Highly successful people have their antennae up all the time. They listen for information that pertains to their work. They ask questions that cut right to the heart of the matter. After receiving the information they need, they say thanks and go on their way. Such behavior need not be curt or unfriendly. Being brief doesn't mean being offensive.

❧ What You Can Do ❧

As you go through the next few days at work, keep your eyes peeled for opportunites to have productive contacts with co-workers.

1. Make a list of the important conversations you need to have with other people that you've been putting off. For example, you may need to discuss a problem you've been having with one of your co-workers.

2. Choose one conversation and decide what you want to accomplish with it. Plan what you want to say. Rehearse exactly the words you will use in opening the conversation, what you'll say in the middle, and how you will end it. Imagine what the other person might say and think. Conduct a practice conversation in your mind.

3. Conduct the actual conversation. If it's really a crucial situation, find a trusted colleague or confidant and try it out live. Afterward, ask yourself if you accomplished what you wanted to. What went well? What would you do differently next time?

4. If you find yourself on the receiving end of a key moment, do what you can to cooperate with the other person. Listen carefully. Present your ideas and responses clearly. Try to work together to reach a positive conclusion.

5. Don't be discouraged if you don't meet your goals in one sitting. Sometimes two or three brief encounters can get you to your goals more effectively than one longer conversation. That gives you and the other person time to think things through before coming to a conclusion or solution.

6. If there are multiple topics you want to discuss with someone, write them down so that you won't get distracted and forget to cover an important issue.

 ## Tips from the Highly Successful

• **Walk in the other person's shoes.** If you're having trouble imagining how the other person would respond to you, set aside your mental rehearsal for a few moments. Instead, imagine that you are the other person. How does this situation look from his or her point of view? What are the person's concerns? What does he or she want to happen?

• **Stay on your feet.** When you hold a stand-up conversation, it's clear that you're not settling in for a long discussion.

• **Look and listen for connections.** If you are talking to the right people and discussing work activities, it's hard not to pick up useful information that helps you to do a better job.

• **Begin at the end.** It often helps to first let people know what you want and then explain why. Tell the other person your conclusion, then review how you got there. This puts your comments in some framework instead of making the other person try to figure out where you are going with the discussion.

- **Watch your timing.** A good time for you to have a brief meeting may be the worst time for someone else. It's easy to begin with, "Say Mary, is this a good time to talk about . . . ?" Pay attention to any hesitation or a lukewarm response.

Chapter 11

Think of Every Meeting
as Your Own

I n 1957 I went to UCLA as a graduate student and research assistant. We were studying groups and their behavior. Until that time I had always placed the responsibility for the success or failure of a meeting squarely on the person who was leading it. But when I objectively observed meetings, it was obvious that a skillful group of participants could make a meeting go well, despite an inept leader. People could really run meetings from "second place." And the best leader was powerless against a group of self-centered people who would not let go of their own hidden agendas.

I was introduced to the simple but powerful fact that meetings take place at two levels—content and process. The content was all about ideas, facts, information, problems, and decisions. The process was like putting on a face mask and looking into the ocean. You suddenly saw a teeming underworld of emotions and people sparring with each other. The mechanics of effective meetings and the real forces that often dictated decisions were revealed. Managing both content and process was a huge job, more than any one person could usually handle.

I awakened to the fact that meetings succeed when everyone makes "leadership" contributions. Not all the direction needed can ever come from any one person.

Whether you're the official leader or a participant in a meeting is less important than whether or not you're committed to making the meeting highly productive.

A lot of people hate meetings. Not highly successful people. They know how to make the most of meetings, whether they're leaders or participants, by:

• Showing up on time with all the appropriate papers.

• Knowing before they go into a meeting what they want to get out of it.

• Paying attention to other people and their ideas.

• Speaking up, and encouraging others to do the same.

• Making their points with both facts and opinions—and being clear about which is which.

• Not confusing loudness with logic.

• Cooperating, not competing.

• Helping keep the meeting on track, even if they're not the leader.

• Nailing decisions down as they go.

• Making every effort to get meetings to start and stop on time.

• Insisting on clarifying assignments before the meeting ends.

        In the old days, meetings were usually led by whoever was highest on the totem pole. Today, everybody leads meetings, often jointly. You can't just sit back and depend on someone else to keep things moving along. You've got to jump in and help make it happen yourself.

If you don't know how to get the most out of meetings, you're in for everything from ineffective social gatherings to eye-glazing, time-sucking, truly lost moments (or hours) in your workday.

☙ What You Can Do ❧

Go to meetings. Every meeting you attend is a chance to become better at leading and participating in meetings.

1. Write down the outcome you want from an upcoming meeting. Don't be too ambitious. The most useful outcomes to shoot for are modest and concrete. Some examples: (a) a new order entry form, (b) a better understanding of a report's major findings, (c) a list of ideas for how to solve an overtime problem. Before the meeting, share your expectations. See what the others think.

2. Ask for an agenda for an upcoming meeting or offer to help put one together.

3. Think in advance about what you should bring to the meeting. Always bring your calendar, to-do lists, or whatever information might be useful.

4. Volunteer to take notes at a meeting. Taking notes forces you to pay attention. It also gives you a way to contribute in addition to offering your ideas.

5. During a meeting, summarize the discussion from time to time. For example: "It sounds like we're moving in the direction of requesting a new printer. Is that right?" Frequent summaries keep everyone focused and clear up potential misunderstandings.

6. Before a meeting ends, make sure that everyone agrees on what was decided, what the action items are, who is responsible for them, and by when. You may need to insist gently that people take the time to do this. At the end of some meetings, people are thinking only of escape.

7. Don't assume silence means consensus. If people are quiet, ask them what they're thinking.

8. Volunteer to facilitate a meeting. That takes pressure off the person who normally does it and gives you good experience.

 Tips from the Highly Successful

• **Take the group's temperature.** Even if they say nothing, people in meetings can be counted on to occasionally become tired, confused, restless, or upset. Tune in to these occasions. Some things you can say to get people back on track:

"Are you all tracking here? I'm confused."
"Is anyone else brain-dead besides me? How about a two-minute break?"
"We seem to be at an impasse. Any ideas on how to move forward?"

• **Write up your notes ASAP.** If you're responsible for writing up the notes for what happened at a meeting, don't wait until right before the next meeting. Schedule time as soon as the meeting is over. The details will be fresher in your mind. If you are not responsible for the meeting minutes, do this for your own reference. Don't stick your scribbled notes in a file; copy them down in a way that will make sense later to you or to someone else. File the clean copy and throw out your original notes.

• **Get graphic.** If you've got facts and figures to present, how about preparing some charts or graphs? They don't have to be elaborate, just clear. You might want to draft one or two and try them out on other people before the meeting.

• **Bring handouts.** If you're going to use handouts, bring extra copies for additional people who may attend or those who forgot to bring theirs.

Chapter 12

Overcommunicate

One summer I worked in the shipping department of a steel mill. My job was to be sure the structural steel had been inspected and then arrange to have it put on railroad cars and sent to the customers. It was totally different from anything I had ever encountered and the training I got was way too brief. One day one of the old hands in the office handed me a shipping order form and said, "Send this order out." On top of the form there was a company name to which we'd sent some previous orders, so I proceeded to verify that the steel had been inspected and then shipped out several tons of structural steel just as I'd done before.

Two days later, my supervisor inquired about the order. I said I'd already shipped it out and happened to name the city where it was going. A look of horror came over his face. "Oh, no, that's the wrong location," he groaned. This customer had two major facilities and the order was for a destination I didn't know existed. The goof was compounded by the fact that the right destination was east and the train with the steel on it was headed west. It was an expensive mistake.

So what happened? Everything my co-worker said to me was correct. He just didn't go far enough. And I should have known that big corporations have more than one location. I should have confirmed the destination. This was one of those classic communication foul-ups that well-intentioned people commit every day. The trouble was that both the company and the customer paid the price for our communication snarl.

Work has changed a great deal in the past 20 years. It used to be that people could do their jobs and keep pretty much to themselves. They got by with a John Wayne "yup" or "nope" style of interacting with others, because their work was done in isolation. Farmers, artisans, and factory workers didn't need to communicate all that much with others. Then everything changed. Now we're living on an information superhighway. One person's work is highly intertwined with many other people's. The communication that used to be a luxury has now become a necessity. The problem is, many people haven't yet gotten the message about the need to act differently.

If you're like most of us, you think that, although you communicate enough, *other* people need to communicate more.

Why don't we communicate more? Because we assume other people already know what we know. Because we think communicating something once is enough. Because communicating takes time away from our "real work." Because we don't stop to think about how important it is for others to know what we know. Because we prefer to communicate only good news and hide problems under the rug.

All of the above reasons (or excuses) for not communicating more are understandable, but they throw sand in the gears of the best organizations. Today's organization demands that people keep each other well informed.

Highly successful people make a point of keeping other people informed every step of the way.

• They let others know of current problems or potential problems down the road.

• They give periodic progress updates—even if they have no progress to report.

- Sometimes they check in simply to review what's going on.

To some people, all this communicating can seem like overkill. To the highly successful, it's barely enough. That's because in today's organizations people work on many different projects with many different people, frequently in different locations. With

> **Keeping others informed is not just a nice idea. It's a key part of your job.**

such busy schedules, people need constant updating about what's happening and what needs to be done, when, and by whom.

> **Peter Drucker, famed management consultant and author, said, "It is not enough to simply do a good job. You have to let other people know you are doing a good job." It's also important to let people know when you haven't done a good job.**

Many people have a hard time grasping the fact that communicating to others about important issues—the status of a project, a call from an unhappy customer, a machine that's not working properly—is as much part of their job as finishing a drawing, completing a report, or shipping out the materials.

Highly successful people are straightforward about communicating their mistakes. They know that disclosing their mistakes saves others from unpleasant surprises and sets the stage for doing it right the next time. Telling others about mistakes also builds credibility. People will believe what you tell them when they see that you're an absolutely straight shooter.

> **There are times when it's important to say you have nothing to say, just to let the other person know you haven't forgotten or tuned out.**

⚙️ What You Can Do ⚙️

Almost all of us could communicate more in virtually every area of our work.

1. If you're involved in carrying out a change of some kind—an improvement in how you do your work, for example—let others know. Tell them what you're doing, why it's important, and how they'll be affected. Afterward, check in frequently to see how they're doing.

2. When you're working on a project, prepare a project update. List key developments since your last communication. Don't forget to communicate lack of progress as well.

3. If there's a rumor floating around that you think could stir up trouble, try to get to the bottom of it. Ask your manager about it. Do your part to clarify what's truth and what's error.

4. Communicate your whereabouts. If you have voice mail, update your announcement every day. "I'm sorry I can't take your call right now, please leave a message," isn't very informative. Have you stepped away for a minute? Are you on a three-day business trip? Get more specific: "Hello, today is April 12, and I'll be in meetings all morning. I'll

listen to your message this afternoon." Announcements like this let callers know what to expect.

5. If someone leaves you a message asking for information (or some other request), and you're working on it, don't wait until you've finished to respond. Let the person know you got the message. Say,"I'm working on it," and state when you expect to get back to them with an answer.

 Tips from the Highly Successful

• **Value mistakes, but don't repeat them.** A mistake-free life is a good indication you're not trying anything new. At the same time, learn from your mistakes. Never make the same mistake twice.

• **Select the right medium.** Should you communicate orally or in writing? If your message contains a lot of complicated information, put it in writing. If it's short, or if you want to get immediate feedback, have a discussion. Also, what would the recipient prefer: A conversation? Memo? Voice mail?

Incidentally, even if you plan to deliver spoken information, consider writing it down first. The process of writing is clarifying. Some people don't know what they want to say until they write it down.

• **Communicate up, down, and all around.** In the old days employees had to communicate through official channels: up to the boss and then down to employees. Today those channels are breaking down. So if you need to communicate to someone in another department, send the message straight to him or her.

If your message is positive, put it in writing and copy the world. If it's corrective, negative, or a mistake that must be put in writing, limit distribution to protect the self-esteem of those involved.

- **Outline complex requests.** If you're the recipient of a complex or complicated message, outline the request as you understand it and ask the sender to confirm that you've got it right.

Chapter 13

Don't Play the
Blame Game

I was the cofounder of a company that provides consulting and training to other organizations. At one point we experienced a rash of errors in the shipment of our products to our customers. My first impulse was to run down to the shipping department and confront the people who pick and pack the orders: "What's the matter with you folks? Can't you get the right things in a box?" But in addition to being a terrible approach to dealing with people, it would have been extremely unfair.

When we dug into the problem, it became clear it was quite complex. Each time you thought you understood the cause of the problem, when you dug deeper you found it had deeper roots. Yes, the people who did the picking and packing made some errors. But far more were made by customers not understanding what they were going to get when they placed an order. That was caused by the sales force not making it clear to the customers exactly what they would be receiving. The sales force also made their share of mistakes in placing orders. That confusion came from some of our marketing material that was unclear and did not describe exactly what customers would receive. Our product development group gave similar names to different products, and this confusion caused some of the errors. Not all items had been precisely numbered and coded to allow the people doing the picking and packing to know exactly what was being ordered.

The big "aha" to me personally was that this seemingly simple problem of customers not getting what they wanted had roots that went into virtually every area of our company. No *one* was to blame. We were all responsible for the problem.

A big drag on high performance is spending time figuring out *who's* wrong versus *what's* wrong. Years ago I was consulting with a company that had extremely talented, well-trained people. Strangely, very little seemed to get done. People spent lots of time writing memos to file and pulling together extensive "just-in-case" documents. If you saw someone smiling in the midst of some difficult problem, you knew that person had figured out who to blame for the problem. The company was a prime example of the saying, "It doesn't matter whether you win or lose, it's how you place the blame."

In that organization, figuring out who was to blame for something was more important than being productive and getting something done. Because the punishment for doing something wrong was so great and the rewards for doing something well were so small, good people began to do less and less. The blame game was a major barrier to productivity.

Research by the pioneers of the total quality movement shows that in the average organization 80 percent of problems are caused by glitches in "the systems." Only 20 percent are caused by personal errors.

It may not make much sense to spend time blaming people when things go wrong, because 80 percent of the time the problem lies elsewhere.

In fact, even when it doesn't, it doesn't pay to blame people. Think about how you feel when you get blamed for something—even if you deserve it. Does it make you want to do better? Cooperate more? Probably not.

> **Being able to accept negative criticism is one of the characteristics of a mature adult. However, criticism can bring out the child in all of us. Unless it is done in the proper way, at the right time, it can backfire. And if we think we're being blamed unfairly, we may do our best to act cool, but we'd really like to punch the critic in the nose.**

Still, we can all improve our performance. We all do things we need to know about so we can avoid doing them again. So what's the answer?

Highly successful people have discovered that the secret is to focus not on the person, but on the issue or behavior involved.[1] What's the difference? More than you might think. Consider the following responses.

Focus on the Person	Focus on the Issue or Behavior
"You are a sloppy word processor."	*"I found five spelling errors in this report."*
"You people in MIS just love to make life complicated and embarrass me in front of the executive committee."	*"We need to find a faster way to get current sales data to the executive committee."*
"Stop being so lazy and read the manual for a change!"	*"The two middle steps in the process have been left out. I think you'll find them in the manual."*

---

1. This is one of five basic principles that are the foundation for all Zenger Miller programs. They have been taught to hundreds of thousands of team leaders, supervisors, and managers. For a complete list of the Basic Principles see Appendix 1.

When you switch focus from the person to the behavior, you'll notice several benefits:

• You'll have to get more specific: "Current sales data," "two steps," "five spelling errors." This will make your comments more helpful to the other person.

• You'll need to observe more carefully. This will keep you honest.

• You'll avoid sweeping statements that start with "you always . . ." or "you never . . ." This will keep you from making the other person angry as soon as you open your mouth.

• You'll use fewer words like "should" and "have to." This will keep you from sounding like a know-it-all.

Some people are too angry and too hurried to take this approach. Others think it's too "nicey-nice." They assume they have to lay it on the line, so the other person gets it. They may even believe the other person deserves to be personally criticized.

> **In the long run, does it really matter whose fault something is?**

Highly successful people, on the other hand, recognize the advantages of taking a less personal approach:

• The other person doesn't get defensive. This makes life easier all around.

• Because the focus is on the facts, less time is wasted in unproductive arguing about who did what, who's right, and who's wrong.

• Time spent fixing blame is better spent fixing problems.

• Relationships are preserved. Both parties can continue to work together without past resentments getting in the way.

• When people don't fear they'll be blamed, they're usually more open about examining—and improving—their own behavior.

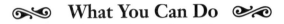

What You Can Do

What the speaker may mean as a neutral statement, the listener may hear as blaming. So it's a good idea to go out of your way to keep your statements blame-free.

1. The next time something goes wrong, try to spot the problem in the process and not the person involved. For example, avoid saying, "Those people in order processing always mess things up." Instead, look for disconnects in the order fulfillment process that are causing problems. What are they? How can they be fixed?

2. Go for a day without blaming anybody for anything—at work or at home. This may not be as easy as you think. A lot of statements only *seem* to be blame-free. Example: "Well, it certainly isn't *my* fault!" (unspoken thought: "but it is somebody else's").

3. Don't criticize people behind their backs. Even though grapevines are part of organizational life, do your part to keep gossip to a minimum. Find some other way to bond with your co-workers.

4. When you are asking questions to identify the problem, avoid the words "how" and "why," which

tend to make people defensive. ("Why did market-ing do that?" "How did you place the order?") In-stead, begin questions with words like "what," "where," "when," and "how much." ("What factors led to that decision?")

5. Begin difficult conversations by diverting blame. "I'm certain there were many things out of your control in this situation. I'm trying to figure out how to fix this problem once and for all. Could you help me understand what happened from your viewpoint?"

 ## Tips from the Highly Successful

• **Avoid beginning sentences with "you" for a while.** To get in the habit of not focusing on the person, try to avoid "you" sentences, as in, "You didn't get the information you promised for the report." Try "we," if it makes sense: "We don't have the information we need for the report."

• **Not blaming is contagious if you wait long enough.** Once people realize they're not being blamed any more, their own behavior will change and they'll start blaming less. But be patient; it may take awhile.

• **Take a similar approach when acknowledging your own mistakes.** Own up to your mistakes, but focus on solving the problem or keeping it from happening again, not beating your-self up.

Chapter 14

Look Out for Number 2 . . . and 3 and 4 and 5

When I was a boy, some friends and I built a tree house. It was no architectural marvel, but it served our purposes and didn't fall down. Looking back on that experience, what stands out for me now is that no one told us what to do. We just all pitched in and did it. There was no boss. No one felt like a subordinate. And that partially accounts for how much fun it was, and how hard we all worked on it.

When I began working with organizations, it was assumed people needed supervisors to tell them what to do—and to make sure they did it right. What's more, most "experts" believed that supervisors couldn't supervise more than eight subordinates. That is, we needed lots of bosses.

It's taken decades for pioneering organizations to prove that what worked for kids building a tree house also works in organizations: with the right preparation, people working in teams can manage themselves and do it better, faster, and cheaper than the old military command-and-control mode.

Today, in fact, there's a new hero in modern organizations.

Out is the superstar who singlehandedly saves the day. In is the
team player, the man or woman who works with other people
to produce better results than anybody could produce on his or
her own.[1]

> **In more and more organizations today, teams of employ-
> ees do real work, make real decisions, and produce
> real results. Today, in fact, it's not unusual for teams to
> manage themselves.**

Teams and teamwork are facts of organizational life today.
Automation helped some organizations get to the 10-yard line, but
teams are responsible for the touchdowns. Highly successful people
know that in this new world, being productive means working
hard to guarantee everybody's success, not just their own.

They also know that teamwork brings with it new
expectations and behaviors.

• Group decisions can take longer and seem messier than
decisions made by one person. But—and it's a big "but"—
they're usually wiser, and are carried out more successfully,
because more of the people involved helped shape them.

• The most effective teams often involve people from several
departments, because these teams can handle all those thorny
interdepartmental issues.

• A team that always agrees on everything is just as bad as a
team that agrees on nothing. Highly successful people have

---

1. This is the third Basic Principle on which all Zenger Miller programs are
based. See Appendix 1.

learned how to stand up for what they think is right without stalling progress. When you do that, the quality of decisions goes way up, and work becomes fun because you are truly making a difference.

✋ What You Can Do ✋

If you're already on a team, you may have had training in skills like problem solving, group decision making, giving feedback, and handling conflicts. Even if your organization doesn't have teams, there are still things you can do to encourage more team-work within your group and among departments.

1. Sponsor a team-building activity. For example, you could set up a get-acquainted lunch or coffee-and-doughnut session to introduce a new employee in your work group or department. Schedule a time to get everyone's idea on a prob-lem the group has been wrestling with.

2. Look at an interdepartmental issue from the other department's point of view. Try to imagine how its members would see the situation. For example, if you have a problem with the people in purchasing, they may also be having a problem with you. How do you think *they* would describe the situation? What do you think they might expect from *you?* It's amazing how accurately a group can predict another group's feelings if they just take the time to think about them.

3. Give others information about how they're doing. The more information people have about their per-formance, the easier it is for them to do better.

4. Help someone do better. These days people have to get coaching or training wherever they can find it. If you have an idea for helping someone improve his or her performance, let them know. You don't have to give a lecture. A suggestion or two will probably get your point across. In fact, research shows that suggesting more than two ideas at a time generates such defensiveness that they fall on deaf ears.

5. Share information about trends and technologies that might affect your group.

6. Talk to other team members about what they do. People on teams need to see the big picture—not just how their work fits into the puzzle, but how everyone fits in.

Tips from the Highly Successful

• **Be patient.** Teams don't become high-performing overnight. It takes time for the members of a team to jell as a cohesive, productive unit. If you're on a new team, expect some ups and downs before you reach cruising altitude.

• **Be tolerant of slips.** Team progress is a bit like walking up a sand dune. People slide back a bit, but don't let that discourage you. Keep seeing the overall progress you're making, and expect some minor slides. Two steps forward and one step back will still get you there.

• **Pitch in.** Don't hold back out of either shyness or a fear that people won't agree with you. A team needs full participation from all members, especially those who have a unique slant on matters.

- **Try saying "we" for a while.** When discussing the work of your group, don't always talk in terms of what "she" did, or "I" did, or "you" did. Try saying "we" whenever you can: "the idea we came up with," for example, "the work we did," or "the problem we ran into."

> **Within organizations today, the word is cooperation, not competition.**

- **Reward all team members equally.** When a team does well, everyone must get rewarded. You'll undermine the team's spirit if you single out one member for recognition.

- **Check your ego at the door.** As people from all levels work together on teams, the distinction between bosses and employees is fading. So don't pull rank (if you've got any) or wave your advanced degrees around (if you've got any). You'll get further by working side by side with everybody else.

- **Abandon the "I'll scratch your back . . ." mentality.** Pitch in when other people need your help, but don't keep score. Don't think of it as doing someone a favor: think of it as contributing to the group's work.

- **Communicate to the entire team.** There's great benefit in conveying important information to all team members at the same time. It prevents misunderstandings and minimizes widely different interpretations.

- **Celebrate small successes.** Keep your team welded together and in high spirits by recognizing progress. Don't wait to cross the finish line. Rejoice over each milestone.

PART THREE
HOW TO MANAGE YOURSELF AND YOUR FUTURE

One of the most profound changes in organizations in the past decade has been the shift from the military model of command and control to an emphasis on people managing themselves. The idea that one person does not need to be controlled by someone else has shaken the roots of old management theory. In years gone by, a cornerstone of management was control. That worked well doing the kind of work people did decades ago.

But today, we know that to achieve high performance we get a great deal further by emphasizing self control. Our work is more complex. More people must be involved. The number of supervisors and middle managers has been reduced. That calls for a level of self-management never before seen. But it will work only if everyone is willing to behave responsibly.

Chapter 15

Be Your Own Boss

It used to be common for fathers and sons to work for the same company. In one case, the father had spent 37 years working in a manufacturing plant. His son now worked in the same plant and went to visit his retired father. The son described the new practices taking place in the plant. Gone were the many layers of management. Gone were the flinty supervisors who barked orders and told people precisely what to do. But most striking to the father was the son's description of how his team was now ordering materials, scheduling production, inspecting their own product, talking with customers, and working directly with equipment suppliers. As the son described these profound changes, tears came to his father's eyes. He said quietly, "We tried to tell them. We knew how to do it all along. No one would listen."

Jack Welch, chairman of GE, wrote: "It is embarrassing to
reflect that for 90 years we've been dictating equipment needs
and managing people who knew how to do things much better
and faster than we did."

Possibly the most profound change in management
theory and practice in the past decade has been the shift from an
emphasis on control by managers, to the concept of self-control
by each person. Many managers have been ready to give up that
control, but people in the organization forgot that their manager
could stop controlling things only when they started to exercise
control over themselves and their work.

In some circles, the term "boss" is no longer politically
correct. We aren't supposed to be—or have—bosses any more.
Instead, we are or have managers, group leaders, team leaders,
or facilitators. (Nevertheless, here we'll use the term "boss" as
shorthand for all of these roles and titles.)

Political correctness aside, these name changes reflect a
real shift in reality. As companies get flatter and leaner, there are
fewer bosses to go around. Instead of six or seven people, it's
not unusual for a manager or leader to have responsibility for
25 people.

Highly successful people respond to this new state of
affairs by:

• Taking more initiative to manage themselves.

• Taking a more active role in working with their bosses.

If you've got a good leader, you're in luck. If you're
unhappy with your leader, don't feel sorry for yourself. You may
not be able to create exactly the leader you want, but you can
certainly make the most of the one you've got.

Highly successful people have learned that by following a few basic rules, they can enjoy productive relationships with their immediate superiors. They also keep these rules in mind when dealing with the people who report to them.

Rule #1. Your boss is not your mother or father.

Highly successful people don't expect their bosses to do their work, listen to constant complaints, nag them to meet deadlines, or prod them to clean up their work areas. Nor do they expect unconditional support or special favors. The best bosses don't ever play favorites. They don't give breaks to one person that they can't give to everyone.

Rule #2. Your boss is paid to obtain results, and that means being accountable for your performance.

Your boss does have several responsibilities toward you. In addition to administrative responsibilities, it's your boss's job to:

• Give you advice on how to handle people and situations.

• Run interference, remove obstacles, and line up resources for you.

• Offer feedback on how well you're doing and coaching to help you improve.

• Give you information to help you manage your career.

You can and should make demands on your boss to help you succeed. Still, no boss is perfect. That's why there is Rule #3.

Rule #3. It's up to you to make the most of the boss you've got.

Overall, does your boss seem to make your life more difficult? Or would you say he or she is interested in helping you do better?

If you have a difficult boss, act as if you had a demanding customer. Demanding customers are focused on what you're giving them. They're less interested in how you do it.

To get the most from a difficult boss:

• Make sure you know exactly what your boss expects of you. Clarify these expectations on a daily basis if necessary.

• Don't take it personally. Don't let a critical boss demolish your self-esteem.

• Think of your primary job as satisfying these expectations and exceeding them, if possible.

• Keep your boss informed of progress—and lack of progress. Be the one to initiate contact.

• Find out the pressures your boss operates under, and do what you can to help him or her deal with them.

• Don't burden your boss unnecessarily with your problems.

• Don't push for more of a personal relationship than your boss wants.

Keep in mind that many difficult bosses are simply pushing you to do a better job.

If your boss is the kind of person who plays a more direct role in helping you do a better job, you're lucky. Treat him or her like an expensive trainer or coach you've hired to help you improve your golf game or control your weight.

To make it easy for your boss to give you honest feedback:
- **Ask for feedback frequently.**
- **Don't get defensive. Just listen; don't explain or justify.**
- **Don't overreact. Nobody will give you honest feedback if they think you're going to be in a blue funk as a result—or immediately ask for a raise.**
- **Show appreciation for the feedback.**

To get the most from a coaching boss:

• Be as open as possible about your strengths and weaknesses.

• Make it as easy as possible for your boss to give you honest feedback. (If you hired an expensive personal trainer, wouldn't you want to get the very most for your money?)

• Ask for help. Don't expect your boss to solve your problems—that's your job—but do ask for help in how to approach a problem or think through a difficult situation.

• Make a point of observing how your boss handles difficult situations. Try his or her behavior on for size.

• Take a stab at solving the problem yourself and then getting feedback from your boss on what he or she thinks of the solution you've come up with. Your boss will appreciate not being pulled into the problem and see that you are capable of taking action

yourself, yet not exceeding your authority when you seek
approval for the final decision.

Of course, most bosses are difficult at times and helpful
at others, so in the final analysis you may need to apply all
these guidelines.

◎๏ What You Can Do ๏◎

There are several steps you can take to get the most from your
boss.

1. The next time you have a meeting with your boss,
   bring a written list of what you want to cover.
   When you're done, leave. Bosses are busy (or they
   should be!). So make your time together pleasant
   and productive, but don't drag it out.

2. Remind your boss of any pending decisions he or
   she needs to make. Because bosses are busy, if
   they're holding up you or your team, remind them
   nicely. Top performers press their bosses to make
   these decisions.

3. Recognize your boss's efforts. People sometimes
   withhold recognition because they think bosses
   don't need it or would discount it as a cheap
   attempt to gain favor. Not true. Bosses are people,
   too. Compliment them on things they do well. Let
   your leader know how he or she can be more
   effective with your colleagues.

4. If your boss seems overextended, volunteer to take
   on a task or two. It's a good way for you to learn.

And maybe you'll free up your boss's time to go
to bat on an issue that's important to you.

5. Track your commitments to your boss. Write down
   on your calendar or personal organizer what you
   commit to do.

6. Tell your manager what you need and why. Don't
   wait for your leader to ask if you need equipment,
   materials, time, or a rearranging of priorities. In a
   perfect world, your leader might see your need.
   But don't count on it. The leader is there to help
   overcome obstacles, not read your mind.

7. Anticipate what others need. If you know something will be needed from you, don't wait to be
   asked. Volunteer your help.

 ## Tips from the Highly Successful

• **Take the initiative.** Don't wait for your boss; he is probably
waiting for you. Don't assume your boss is completely on top of
your work. She has other things to worry about. It's always up to
you to initiate meetings, issue reminders, and follow through on
your deadlines.

• **Never surprise your boss.** Don't withhold bad news in the
hopes that "something will happen" before your boss learns
about it. Let your boss know what to expect at the earliest
possible moment. Tell him or her what you're doing about it.

• **Be a low-maintenance employee.** People don't usually keep
high-maintenance cars around for very long. The same is true for

high-maintenance employees. Make sure you're not the kind of employee who takes up more than a fair share of your boss's time and attention.

Chapter 16

Banish Gloom

I had just been hired as the vice president of human resources by Alex Zaffaroni, the president of Syntex Laboratories. He was a chemist by training, and in our first conversation he said, "I know this isn't a highly sophisticated, psychological analysis of people, but I find there are basically two types in the world. There are positive people and there are negative people. I don't enjoy being around negative people, so I hope you'll help us find positive people to work here."

I've thought about his comment many times since. Unlike Alex, I did have formal education in psychology and human behavior. But his analysis is as useful as any I've read in psychology texts. The most productive people in every organization have these characteristics in common: they are fundamentally positive, upbeat, optimistic, and cheerful people.

Highly successful people make a point of being cheerleaders at work. They encourage others.

> **Oscar Wilde observed that people are either "tedious" or "charming."**

They have an eye out for things they can appreciate and celebrate. And they stifle their impulses to whine.

It's not that they're mindlessly positive, or just trying to be "nice." They're trying to be effective. They know productivity rises when the atmosphere at work is positive and constructive and people are easy and even fun to work with. They also know people repeat behavior that is rewarded and abandon behavior that is ignored.

So what's the payoff from such cheerleading?

- It lifts people's self-esteem.
- It encourages people to try new ideas.
- It cements relationships.
- It supports the organization.

Lifting People's Self-Esteem[1]

People do their best work when they feel accepted and valued. They're also more likely to express new ideas and try out new ways of doing things if they don't think they'll be criticized

---

1. Maintaining and enhancing other's self-esteem is another of the Basic Principles that undergird all Zenger Miller programs. For the complete list, see Appendix 1.

for trying. Jack Welch, the chairman of GE, speaks often of the need to build self-confidence from top to bottom in the organization. Self-confident people are the innovators.

Looking for efforts worth cheering about? Here are a few that often go unrecognized:
>   **Standing up for an unpopular idea**
>   **Helping the group reach consensus**
>   **Resolving a dispute**
>   **Trying out a new skill**
>   **Admitting a mistake**
>   **Sharing credit with others**

The secret to making others feel good about themselves is to be specific and honest. Nobody is fed hogwash for long without feeling manipulated. On the other hand, everybody likes sincere and thoughtful recognition. So:

• Pay close attention to what other people are doing that contributes to your group or organization.

• Acknowledge when people do "little" things you know are difficult for them—speaking up in a meeting, for example, or confronting a co-worker.

• Explain *why* something is important. Don't stop with "I like your idea for the new billing format." Say: "because it's going to make it a lot easier for us to answer customer questions."

Encouraging People to Try New Ideas.

A new idea is fragile. It has to be nurtured and protected. Like any young bird or animal, in the first weeks of its life it needs protection from those who would do it harm.

> Some people argue that they were born with a negative attitude and can't do anything about it. However, there's lots of evidence to suggest you can influence how you're feeling inside. If you *act* more positive, you'll begin to *feel* that way.

Cementing Relationships.

Criticizing other people or groups behind their backs is not only unkind, it's unproductive. The days when people worked mostly in their own departments are on their way out. Today we need everyone's full cooperation.

Highly successful people go out of their way not to criticize others behind their backs. They say things like:

- "Let's lighten up on engineering. We need their help."

- "This is new for Ted. You remember what it was like when *you* first started out."

- "The wonderful thing about working with Nancy is the way she encourages you just by how she listens."

> Warner Bros.' animators would meet to flesh out ideas for new cartoons in what they called a "Yes session." Positive comments only—nothing negative allowed. Some of their most creative thinking was born from this restriction on what could be said.

Supporting the Organization

This can be tricky. The people who lead organizations make mistakes. Blindly supporting everything is neither wise nor necessary. But worse yet is the person who is negative about everything the organization does.

The organization has a right to expect that you'll give it the benefit of the doubt. If you're not clear why something has happened, assume it was done for good and logical reasons. Believe the best until proven otherwise.

Most organizations are trying to improve. They embark on programs of total quality management, reengineering, or work process improvement. These are usually sincere attempts to help the organization get better. There are always cynics who remember that 25 years ago the organization tried a program that failed and go around predicting that this new initiative is bound to fail also. These negative people's gloomy views too often become self-fulfilling prophecies. Successful change is never executed by them. It is always the product of the positive people.

Highly successful people take the time and energy to learn about these initiatives. They do their best to figure out what's in it for them and for their co-workers. They share what they've learned and focus on the positive outcomes.

If they can't be supportive, they get out of the path of the people who can. And they look for ways they can get more involved as time goes on.

◈ What You Can Do ◈

You can't will yourself to feel positive. However, you can start looking for things to feel positive about. You can choose to do and say things that emphasize the pros rather than the cons. You can choose to keep negative thoughts to yourself. You can decide to act in a positive way. When you do, you'll begin to feel more positive inside.

1. Observe your co-workers and identify things they do that contribute to the productivity of your group. Tell each person specifically what you have observed. Explain the importance of what they did. Smile, look the person in the eye, and say thanks.

2. If you're involved in a team project, don't wait until the end to recognize team members' efforts. Let them know now how valuable their contributions are.

3. If your group is struggling with an initiative like quality improvement, identify a positive outcome, such as fewer rework problems. If possible, quantify it. ("We'll save an hour a day we used to spend trying to get that machine to work right.") Share your thinking with other people.

 Tips from the Highly Successful

• **Beware the "yes, but."** We often unwittingly undercut praise with criticism. For example: "You're such a creative letter writer. It's too bad you make so many spelling mistakes."

• **Avoid backhanded compliments**. If you're going to recognize someone's behavior, make sure you're sincere. Don't give "compliments" like, "You know, for an accountant you write really well."

• **"They" didn't make you do it.** If you're called upon to explain an organizational policy or program to other people, don't say things like "Management thinks it's a good idea to . . ." or "They want us to . . ." It makes you sound powerless. Instead, jump right up on the bandwagon. Try saying "It makes sense to . . ." or "If we do this, then we'll be able to . . ."

• **Put up. Then shut up.** If you have strong objections to a program, make them known. Once you've been heard—and understood—either get with it or keep quiet. You don't want to be the bad apple that spoils the whole barrel.

• **Poke fun at yourself, not others.** Nothing gets leaders in more trouble than attempts to be funny that backfire. Guard against barbed remarks or sarcasm that puts others down.

Chapter 17

Monitor the Money

W hen you take a small child shopping with you, it is not unusual to hear, "I want that wagon," "I want an ice cream cone," or "buy me a balloon."

Children view their parents as a source of unlimited funds to be spent in making them happy. As children grow up, they realize resources are limited. Then when they have children of their own, you witness that wonderful cycle in which they develop an entirely new perspective on buying things, the value of money, and their role in managing family finances.

When people start working for a company they often go through a similar maturing process. They may initially see the organization as having vast financial resources that someone else worries about. How the money gets used is not their concern as long as they get everything that they need or that makes their life more comfortable.

When it comes to their organization's financial health, too many people have their heads in the sand. They think finance is too complicated to understand. Besides, they say, why bother? Worrying about money and budgets is for someone in accounting or finance, or several layers above me in the organization.

Highly successful people know differently.

• First of all, they know there is a direct link between the financial well-being of an organization and every employee in it. In fact, no link is *more* direct.

• Second, they know the leaders of their organization pay close attention to the numbers. It's how they know whether or not they're doing a good job. It's part of your job to evaluate everything that goes on in terms of its impact on the bottom line, whether you are a CEO or a customer service rep.

So if you want to know what the executives in your organization are thinking about—and why—be a leader and learn something about the numbers yourself.

Financial measures aren't the only numbers that count. Operational efficiency and measures of quality are extremely important. But even if those numbers are terrific, when the financial numbers are bad for long periods of time your company could find itself out of business. Financial measures are truly the bottom line.

How's *your* organization doing? Turning a profit? Doing better than it did last year, or worse? What about your department or work group? If you don't know, find out. You'll make better decisions if you do.

To understand what's behind the numbers, highly successful people make it a point to follow the money, starting with the budget for their department or work group.

First, they learn how money is accounted for. They understand how expenses differ from capital expenditures and how big an item must be for it to be capitalized. What tests must it meet?

Once you've learned how money is tracked, find out if it is spent wisely.

Most departments have budgets. How is your department doing against its budget right now? Is it under? Over? In what areas? If it is over budget, what can you do to help get spending back on track? In what areas is the budget overspent? Travel, telephone, express shipping, supplies? What can you do to pull things back into line? Do you have any ideas about how your department could save money?

Don't try to fudge and charge expenses where they should not be charged.

∾ What You Can Do ∾

You don't need to be a financial analyst to learn something about your organization's bottom line. Once you start looking for information, you'll be surprised what you pick up.

1. Make sure you understand your group's budget, where you are over and under, and why that's happened. If you're over in an account, find out what's been charged there. Look for items you don't recognize. The accounting department can make mistakes in coding expenses. Or accounting may have disagreed with how you coded an item, and you'll need to discuss it with them.

2. Discuss with your co-workers how you could cut expenses without harming your group's

performance. Start with those budget areas where you are over your budgeted amounts.

3. Identify areas where you could spend a little money to save a great deal more. People in organizations are not rewarded only for saving money. Rewards come to those who spend money in ways that produce positive results.

4. Learn about where your company gets its income. Which products are selling well? Which aren't? Which regions are exceeding their sales goals?

 Tips from the Highly Successful

• **Don't be intimidated.** There may be terms in financial or business reports you don't understand. Don't worry about them; try to get a general sense of what's going on. Brokerage houses give out free booklets on how to read financial reports.

• **Read a book or two.** If you discover that you are interested in financial and business news and want to learn more, do some reading. A good place to start is your local library. There are many books that explain finances to people with no financial background. One is *The 7 Secrets of Financial Success,* by Root and Mortensen, Irwin, 1996. Another is *Personal Finance for Dummies,* by Eric Tyson, published by IDG Books.

• **Keep up to date on company finances.** Read the financial reports or other information your company gives you about its financial condition. More and more organizations regularly provide employees with financial information. Check it out. If you don't understand some terms, ask for help. (This could be a good reason to connect with someone in finance or accounting.)

• **Become an owner if possible.** If your company is publicly traded, follow the stock in your daily newspaper. See if you can spot trends or figure out why it changes value from one day to the next. (To follow your company's stock, you need to know which stock market it is traded on and its abbreviation or symbol).

If your company has an employee stock ownership plan (ESOP), that's an easy, cost-effective way to become an owner. Or purchase some shares yourself from a brokerage firm. They'll give you an additional stake in your organization's success.

Chapter 18

Learn, Learn, Earn

Professor Herb Shephard was one of the founders of the discipline of organization development. I recall him describing a major study he had done for a large aerospace company on the subject of obsolescence of engineers. Company managers observed that many of their engineers were not being productive, while others were making huge contributions. The difference was first thought to be the number of years the employees had been out of engineering school. That did not prove correct. Then they looked at which schools the engineers came from. They could see no pattern. Age didn't make the difference either.

Shephard's conclusion, after an extensive study, was a condition he called "obsolescence of spirit." Some engineers did little to keep current in engineering literature, to take further classes, or to develop new interests. They withered on the job.

Other engineers did just the opposite. They had the urge and the discipline to keep learning. Their minds were curious. They developed new interests. While the young graduates may have had some edge on the latest technology, the experience of older engineers would prevail so long as their spirit had not dried up.

In the future when people talk about the haves versus the have-nots, they may well be referring not to money but to education and training. The earnings gap between professionals and clerical workers has gone from 47 percent to 86 percent in the past 15 years. College-educated males aged 24 to 34 have seen their earnings increase by 10 percent in the past decade. But the earnings of those with only high school diplomas have dropped 9 percent, and those with no high school diploma have had a 12 percent decline in their earnings. To look at it another way, males with 16 years of education outearn those with 12 or less by 60 percent.

It's already happening. Our society develops new industries and jobs for trained and educated people, leaving relatively few higher-paying jobs for the unskilled and the untrained. More than 70 percent of jobs in the future will not require a college degree, yet these jobs are the foundation of our economy. Their productivity will determine our standard of living. The message is clear: If you want to succeed, you've got to learn, learn, learn—not just while you're young, but throughout your life.

There is strong evidence that people who exercise their brains improve their ability to think and solve problems. They also prevent or postpone mental deterioration as they age. Turning off a mindless television program to read a book or even do a crossword puzzle may preserve your brain.

Highly successful people grab every opportunity they can to expand their learning in a wide variety of areas:

- Technical and professional.

- New job skills.

- New technologies, especially computer skills.

- Management skills

- Problem solving, teamwork, process management, and meeting facilitation.

- The bigger economic picture.

- Improved interpersonal skills.

- Breadth of knowledge (learn about industries related to yours, learn about business in general, learn about management even if you're not a manager).

> **The time will soon come when we'll be learning a living.**

Those who really like to learn, not merely get their training tickets punched, are curious and open to new ideas. We used to think of these traits as youthful, but not any more. Go into any community college class, especially in the evenings. You will probably see more senior citizens than twentysomethings.

> **As constant change becomes a way of life in organizations, the job skill with the biggest payoff is the ability to learn—and unlearn, and relearn.**

What do you need to learn? Learning is more than getting more information. That's important, but learning also involves acquiring new skills that ultimately become habits.

What blocks learning? The fact is that many of us stop learning when we leave school. Why? To learn means putting yourself in a childlike position. Others are explaining things to you. You aren't in control. Real learning of any skill often requires making mistakes, and that's embarrassing. Our fear of failure swamps our desire to learn something new.

Note that professions from law to medicine, from dentistry to accounting all require continual education. (Miss them and you lose your license to practice in that profession.) No one can maintain or improve their position in a firm or enhance their productive role without continually honing their skills.

The importance of unlearning. One of the biggest challenges facing people in organizations is to unlearn. The workers who spent years under a boss who punished them for making suggestions now find themselves working with someone who desperately wants their suggestions. That means unlearning old ways and attitudes and erasing the emotional scars left on them by managers who punished rather than praised.

∾ What You Can Do ∾

Organizations today, knowing the value of multiskilled employees, are making more and more training available. But if your organization doesn't, don't let it stop you. Invest in your own future. Check out all possible options: libraries, high schools, colleges and universities, TV educational programs, and correspondence schools. Look for training and information on the World Wide Web.

1. Inventory your skills. What skills do you have? What ones would you like to have? How can you get them?

2. Collect catalogs from your local evening schools and colleges. See what's available. Sign up for a class or seminar to gain new skills or explore areas of interest.

3. Check out your local library's magazine selection. Read a magazine published for people in your current field—or some discipline that would make you even more valuable at work.

4. If you're afraid of computers, bite the bullet and find a course for beginners. Computers are much easier to use than they used to be—and much more common in the workplace. It's never too late to join the information revolution.

5. Become a good problem solver. If you aren't familiar with the proven steps to solving a problem, get a book from your company or public library.

6. Conduct experiments in your job. Ask permission if necessary and then try new ways of doing your job. Track the results. Ask people around you if they have any ideas that you should test.

7. Study history. What worked in the past? What failed? What things did people who had your job before you do? Review minutes of past team meetings or departmental meetings to see what you can learn from both failures and successes.

8. Be an information minstrel. In medieval times, court minstrels traveled from castle to castle carrying the news as they went. Organizations desperately need information carriers.

9. Ask good questions. Listen attentively. Learning is not a spectator sport. It requires activity.

10. Seek learning that is not directly related to your business (cooking, writing, pottery). Pursuing a

variety of interest expands your thinking. Often you can make connections between seemingly unrelated things that change your point of view. In fact, this is really the basis of creativity.

11. Volunteer for projects that allow you to learn new skills.

12. Develop your own personal development plan each year. Set annual goals. Enlist your leader's help in fulfilling them.

"The biggest problem we have around here is that no one can find out what we know."
— **A frustrated executive**

 Tips from the Highly Successful

• **You're surrounded by teachers.** Lots of people in your organization have something to teach you, ranging from advanced training in your own job to basic training in theirs. Today, in fact, many organizations encourage cross-training, in which employees learn each other's jobs. The organization benefits from the flexibility of a cross-trained workforce. You benefit from gaining new skills and being able to add more variety to your workday. You become more marketable. Many organizations reward expanded skills with more money. Even if you don't have a formal cross-training program, find someone in another function who's interested in what you do. Cross-educate each other.

• **Take advantage of what's available to you.** Many organizations support employee training beyond the core required courses. Some pay tuition for certain post-high school courses. Some give you time off to attend classes. Some offer free classes after working hours. Check with your human resources or training department to find out what's available.

• **Ask your boss for suggestions.** Find out from your manager what courses, training, or education would make you a more valuable, productive person in your organization.

• **Make the daily commute a learning opportunity.** Listen to a tape. Whether you are in a car, subway, or train, it's a great time to learn.

• **Accept complete responsibility for your career.** Society does not pressure adults to learn. It's your choice. But the consequences are long-lasting. You must keep running in this race just to keep up with those around you. Snooze and not only you but everyone who depends on you loses.

> **When you say you've finished your education, you're finished. Lifelong learning is a necessity, not a luxury.**

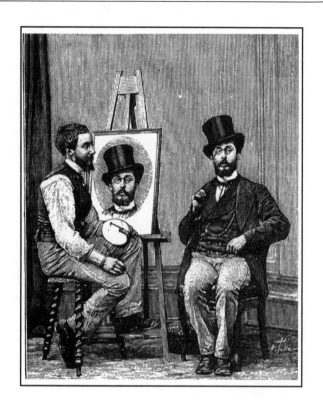

Chapter 19

Multiply Yourself

A new manager had his first meeting with a group of salespeople. There had been much controversy over what was OK to do with clients. How much could you spend for lunch with clients? Could you ever have a drink with them? Could you invite them out for golf? What gifts could you give at holiday time?

Every answer triggered another question. Finally the manager said, "Tell you what. You can do anything you see me do."

In the past 18 chapters we suggested specific things you can do to be highly productive and contribute to your company. But there's something far more powerful about your actions than you may realize. What you do doesn't stop with you. Your example molds others. Like the pebble dropped into a pond, the leader in you causes countless ripples in the organization.

Leadership involves many things. We've discussed them in earlier chapters. Being a good communicator. Striving always to be better. Being optimistic. Contributing to effective team meetings. You can now make a long list. But so what? What's the result?

The outcome of leadership is that *people follow your example.* The leader inside each of us wants to have others watch what we do and follow our example. That's the most powerful thing a leader can do.[1]

What's the best way to make this happen? The most effective leaders do more showing than telling. They set an example of the kind of behavior they want others to follow.

The most powerful examples of effective behavior don't come easily. For instance, if you want everyone to put the customer first, you must do so yourself all the time, not just when it's easy.

It's one thing to say the customer is always right. But if you redo your pet project because customers tell you they don't like it—now *that's* a powerful example.

---

1. This is the fifth Basic Principle on which all Zenger Miller programs are based. See Appendix 1.

By practicing what you preach, you will earn a reputation for credibility. You can more easily:

- Convince others of ideas you think are important.

- Function as an effective team member or leader.

- Earn the trust and respect of your co-workers.

In other words, whether or not you're designated as a manager by your organization, you'll be regarded as a leader by the people who work with you.

In any organization, the front-line people are the most powerful training department. Most real job training happens informally, often indirectly, on the job. Newcomers follow the examples set by the more senior people.

Years ago top management believed that supervisors and middle managers were training new people. It probably wasn't true then, but with the downsizing and flattening of most organizations, it is clear that the real "nuts and bolts" training of new people comes from you. And if you are a person who influences others, then you are the strongest force for shaping the behavior of the people around you.

❧ What You Can Do ❧

Everything you do becomes a model for others to follow. So make sure you're setting a good example—and that your deeds match your words. Here are a few behaviors that will send a strong message to others.

1. Be the best possible citizen of your organization. Understand where it is going. Come to know its customers. Study its financial performance.

2. Master your job. Measure it. Streamline the work processes. Constantly strive to get better. Accelerate the pace. Look for the best performers in the organization and copy them.

3. Manage yourself. Don't be a high-maintenance employee. Don't waste anything, especially time. Display an optimistic, positive outlook at work.

4. Work well with your colleagues. Make brief encounters work. Do your part to make every meeting productive. Be certain that you communicate to those around you. Don't waste time trying to fix the blame, just fix the problem. Look out for your co-workers.

5. Prepare for the future. Keep learning constantly. Be quick to adopt new technology. Get ready for your next job before it becomes available to you.

6. Set a good example. Make certain your deeds exceed your words. Act the way you believe everyone should.

 Tips from the Highly Successful

• **Don't undercut your credibility.** Every time you fail to walk the talk—you say one thing but do another—you lose credibility. Don't take the easy way out. For example, if you think it's important for your team to make group decisions, then don't short-circuit the process when you think they may not make the right one.

• **Behave in the way you'd like everyone to behave.** Some people ask for special exceptions, but that can destroy an organization.

> **Everything you do should pass this simple test: "How would this organization be if everyone did what I am about to do?"**

- **Give credit to others for successes.** Accept responsibility for mistakes and problems. Good leaders pass on credit for success to their co-workers. But if something goes wrong, they accept complete responsibility. It seems like a small thing, but it separates good leaders from bad ones.

- **Boost your productivity.** What we leave our children and grandchildren, and the living standard that we enjoy in the coming years, depend on our ability to become as productive as we can be.

Chapter 20

Get Ready for Your *Next* Job

My father taught me to play checkers and chess. His message was consistent. "Think ahead. Look two or three moves forward. Don't always make your move in response to what I do. You'll never win if you don't make your own plan."

I found that this game wisdom was solid career advice. The early part of my career included working in large corporations, teaching at a university, and then joining Syntex, an international pharmaceutical company. After being there for eight years, I knew I wanted to try the consulting business sometime in the future. So I began publishing articles, taught at the local university, spoke at national conferences, and organized a local group of executives with interests similar to mine. I did this to have options in the future. I was preparing for my next job, yet all the things I did were useful in my current position as well.

It wasn't until three years later that I decided the time was right to leave and start a consulting business. Fortunately it succeeded and evolved into Zenger Miller, a training and consulting business. I was its CEO for 17 years. Then the company was acquired by Times Mirror and now I'm back working inside a large corporation.

After 40 years in the working world, my advice to anyone echoes what my father told me about checkers and chess: think ahead. Make your own career plan. Don't simply respond to what the organization does or offers you.

Check off the statements that best describe how you feel about your current job.

- I love it.

- I hate it.

- I'm getting bored with it.

- I feel secure in it.

- I'm afraid of losing it.

No matter which of these statements you checked, here's one you should also check.

- I'm getting ready for my next job.

That's right. Even if you love your current job and feel secure in it, you should be preparing yourself for your next one.

Why? Lots of reasons. Here are a few.

- Not even the most secure job is completely secure these days.

- Getting ready for another job may be the only time you'll ever stop to assess where you are and where you want to go in your career.

- Getting ready for a job is a great opportunity to learn what's going on in your field outside the confines of your own organization.

Highly successful people are always ready to change jobs if necessary. Partly it's a matter of attitude. They know the realities of the job market, but at the same time they feel confident in their ability to take care of themselves.

They also want to be prepared for the future. Once they land a job, too many people put their noses to the grindstone and never look up. They virtually lose contact with the outside world. This usually doesn't help their performance—and it certainly doesn't help build much of a future for themselves.

We all know loyal, longtime employees who think they can get by on loyalty alone. These are the people who often resist incorporating new technology into their repertoire of job skills. For example:

• The salesperson who never quite gets around to using the laptop computer his company bought to help automate the sales process.

• The marketing communications professional who resists moving beyond the basics of word processing.

• The executive who continues to beg for secretarial assistance instead of taking full advantage of computer programs—personal schedulers, e-mail, groupware, and the like—to work more productively.

Top performers tend to embrace whatever new technologies will help them achieve better results on the job.

All employers are impressed by the people who strive to improve themselves. The people who consistently take classes, participate in internally sponsored training, and pursue degrees or additional coursework

> **Getting ready for your next job can help you perform better in the job you have now.**

are sending a clear message. The status quo is not good enough. They recognize that no matter how bright or skilled they are, they can be better. These are the people who stand out and who capture their bosses' attention. That's why they end up getting the best jobs in the long run.

❧ What You Can Do ❧

Getting ready for your next job doesn't mean you have to apply for jobs or go on job interviews. It's more a matter of keeping yourself up to date on job requirements and market realities.

1. Find out about opportunities within your organization. Read bulletin boards. Talk to people in human resources. Find out what's available now and what's coming up in the future. What qualifications would you need? How would you get them?

2. Read the help wanted ads even if you're not actively looking. It's a good way to find out what kinds of qualifications companies are looking for.

3. Keep up with your friends and work associates. Have lunch. Give them a call from time to time to find out what they're doing and tell them about your activities. Don't wait until you're out of a job to reach out to other people.

4. Take the courses that would be required for you to get the position you'd like. If you don't have anything specific in mind, engage in more general skill development. Nearly every position can benefit from improved writing, math, and computer skills. Learn about spreadsheets, word processing, and groupware that allows teams to function more effectively together.

Tips from the Highly Successful

• **Follow your interests, not just your job requirements.** In time job requirements change and jobs themselves vanish. So don't neglect your interests and abilities. The more you discover and pursue them—and find ways to use them in your work—the happier and more effective you'll be at whatever you do.

• **Keep your resume updated.** As you reach milestones in your work, add them to your resume (or at least to a permanent file you will eventually incorporate into your resume). If you don't actually use your resume for years, all the more reason to keep it updated. It's useful in applying for other positions inside your organization, not only outside opportunities.

• **Seek others' views.** When attending a class or seminar, talk to people about why they are there. What's going on in their organizations? How do they feel about the skill sets they have and need? Hearing about situations outside your organization enlarges your perspective.

• **Cultivate your curiosity.** Take a class just to see what's going on to expand your mind. If you approach it in a less pressured way, you'll be more open to gathering all types of information rather than focusing only on the important facts. You may find your curiosity leading you to yet another area to explore, widening your awareness and knowledge each time.

Chapter 21

Break from the Past

The need for most of us to break with our past is illustrated by an experience I had as a college professor.

In the text we were using I assigned a chapter that I thought was extremely important. I said to the class, "I'd like you to read the supplementary readings at the end of the chapter, and answer the questions that are at the end of the chapter. Hand in your answers at the beginning of our next class. Please be prepared to discuss the supplementary readings. I've put them on reserve in the business school library."

There was a slight pause and a hand shot up. "Sir, do you mean that we're to read *all* of the supplementary readings?"

"Yes, I want you to read them *all.*" There was another short pause.

Another hand came up, "Professor, do you want us to answer every one of the questions—numbers 1 through 8. Even the last two optional ones?" "Yes, I'd like you to answer all of the questions—even the last two listed as 'optional.'"

A low groan came from several members of the class.

School Daze

Schools have created an attitude or norm of getting by with the least effort. Students think, "how little can I do to get the grade I want?" Good grades are often seen only as a doorway to college or graduate school. Learning is seldom for the pure joy of learning.

These high-school and college students are now your co-workers. No miracle changed their mindset. They came into the workplace with the same attitudes they left school with. "What's the least I can do to get by?" While no one person taught them these groundrules, in one sense everyone did. They're just like the air we breathe. They're everywhere, you don't notice it. They surround you.

Something has to put it "in your face" in order to see it clearly. Like the science teacher who vividly demonstrated the "air" that surrounds us via some dramatic demonstration, something equally striking has to occur for us to see that pervasive just-get-by attitude. To change such a widespread attitude requires a strong force. If a company is silent about their expectations, people assume that the old "school days" groundrules hold.

Companies as Accomplices

Companies have done their share to reinforce those attitudes. Autocratic management behavior and the lack of any real participation on the part of the employees reinforced the feeling that management was the "parent" and everyone else the "child." Management practices that treated employees as disposable parts made it worse. The workforce became like a balloon that kept growing larger and larger. Then some executive decided to down-size and stuck a pin into the balloon. People then withdrew, feeling alienated from the company.

And compounding all of that was the hostility that had long existed in some firms between labor and management. That distrust and antagonism strongly encouraged workers to do as little as possible, and on occasion, led to sabotage.

180° Turnabout

This book is about changing all of that. Those old attitudes, beliefs, and behaviors are harmful to everyone involved.

We need to return to even earlier principles and behaviors of our society. As organizations give broader responsibility to each person, the change is like moving from being a galley slave to becoming an old-world artisan. The masons, carpenters, cabinet makers or farmers have always known that their livelihood and their future depended on how well they produced. Period.

That "artisan" mentality—pride in what you produce—needs to be restored. Being willing to stamp your name on the bottom of the silver bowl you produced. That's what this book is about. Doing your best, not "just getting by."

I invite you to examine your attitudes, beliefs, and especially your actions. Be totally honest with yourself. I'm the first to agree that executives need to change many of their attitudes and policies. Many of them are making dramatic changes. But the only person *you* can change is *you.*

The person most credited with the beginning of the total quality management movement is W. Edwards Deming. At the end of many of his speeches given in his final years, he would conclude by saying something like, "I trust that what I have said has been useful to you. *I have done my best."* He would then slowly walk to his seat.

Our world would be a different place if all of us would end each day saying, "I've done my best." We'd win, our companies would prosper, and our nation would rise to new heights.

Let's work at it.

Appendix 1

THE BASIC PRINCIPLES

Focus on the situation, issue,
or behavior, not the person.

■

Maintain the self-confidence
and self-esteem of others.

■

Maintain constructive relationships.

■

Take initiative to make things better.

■

Lead by example.

ZENGERMILLER

Appendix 2

THE ZENGER MILLER PHILOSOPHY

Client Philosophy

*O*ur clients are our colleagues. We will demonstrate our personal respect for their professionalism, dignity, competency, uniqueness, and intelligence. They deserve extraordinary service, support, and concern from us. Our dealings should be ethical, honest, straightforward, and with an uncommon desire to do what is right. Our clients should feel that we are with them for the long run as collaborators in finding practical solutions to organizational change and training needs. We will share with our clients our enthusiasm for increasing individual, managerial, and organizational productivity. Our clients will find us unexpectedly professional, prepared, and committed. They should always feel they have gained significantly from their involvement with us.

Corporate Philosophy

*Q*uality is Zenger Miller's cornerstone value. To us, quality means doing the right things to exceed expectations, doing those things in the right ways, and continually evaluating and improving both what we do and how we do it.

We strive for quality in five areas:

- *Quality products* and services that convey our respect for both our clients and ourselves.

- *Quality results* that will increase productivity, profitability, and long-term fiscal responsibility for our clients and for ourselves.

- *Quality service* that treats our clients with intelligence, responsiveness, efficiency, and courtesy.

- *Quality of life* that allows each of us to use our time in balanced ways to achieve competency, worth, and meaning in our lives.

- *Quality society* that benefits from the use of our abilities to address major social problems and to assist organizations that serve society.

We intend to be a dramatically successful organization in both financial and human performance.

ZENGER MILLER

Associate Philosophy

*Z*enger Miller associates share common values, with quality being at the core. Moreover, we possess and wish to display an uncommon concern for the whole person, going beyond typical relationships in business organizations.

We cherish individual freedom and dignity:
We will safeguard the liberty to challenge and speak out, the liberty to make mistakes and learn, the liberty to be trusted and respected for individual decisions and contributions, and the liberty to do our work without concern for politics, power, or personal entanglements.

We intend to communicate openly:
We want to clearly define mutual expectations, direction, and bedrock values. We desire to give honest and frequent individual feedback, coaching, and recognition for contributions, and to be informed and contribute to overall corporate directions and decisions.

We believe in productivity, balance, and collaboration:
We expect to work hard and achieve high levels of personal and organizational productivity. At the same time, we believe in balanced lives with time for family, community, civic and religious service, and self-improvement.

We do not subscribe to the theory that all wisdom and knowledge are found at the top of an organization, so we strive for informed, responsible, and collaborative decision making in all areas.

We help individual contributors, managers, and executives in client organizations to work more productively and to manage well. We intend to practice what we preach.

Products and Services Philosophy

*O*ur products and services are an expression of our values and philosophy. Whether tangible or intangible, they represent each of us as individuals. We work to develop and sell products and services that do what we say they will do. Our products and services produce desired, lasting results. We use the latest research and learning methodologies, meshed with practicality and usability, to produce products and services that are state-of-the-art, yet workable in the field. We create products and services that treat all people involved with dignity.

INDEX